FOUNDATION

A Guide to Successful & Profitable Writing

(And to everything you didn't learn in English class)

Written by
Barry M. Willis

CRESTINGWAVE
PUBLISHING

FOUNDATION: A Guide to Successful & Profitable Writing
(And to everything you didn't learn in English class.)

Written by Barry M. Willis

Copyright © 2025 Barry M. Willis.
All rights reserved.

For information about the author or to receive copies of the book for review, please send an email to:
pub@gocwpub.com

Edited by Kris Neely
Book Layout: Lazar Kackarovski

Printed in the U.S.A.

First Edition - 2025

ISBN: 978-1-956048-34-6

Published by Cresting Wave Publishing, LLC.

"We publish the books you need to read."

CONTENTS

For Tina Roberts.

ACKNOWLEDGEMENTS

Thanks to Tina Roberts, Laura & Kris Neely, Ken Askew, John Craig Oxford, Rick Clark, Charles McNair, Colleen Bidwill, Vicki Larson, Charles Brousse, Robyn Wiley, Bob Green, Jason Walsh, Linda Xiques, John Atkinson, Jon Iverson, Paul Miller, Mark Levinson, Marcia Tanner, Meredith Tromble, Scott Wilkinson, Joanna Cazden, Stephanie Spadaccini, Lynn White, Andrew Keen, Jesse Beaton & Carl Franklin, Vaughan Acton, and Courtney Grant Winston.

All made an impact; all are hugely appreciated.

Thank you!

INTRODUCTION AND WELCOME TO **FOUNDATION**

You're reading this because you want to be a writer. A better writer. A successful writer.

You're reading this because you want to get a handle on style and substance, or because you want to avoid rookie errors, or because you want to get published and move up through the ranks as quickly as possible. Maybe all three.

Foundation was written with you in mind.

Writers are craftspeople and artists. The empty page is our blank canvas; words are our paints and brushes. With them, we're free to create anything that we wish. That freedom is incredibly empowering.

This book is not an academic treatise. It's not a course in persuasive rhetoric, an examination of 15th-century Italian poetry, or a deep reading of Shakespeare. Those are subjects for graduate school seminars.

Foundation is a compendium about how to deliver maximum impact in accessible contemporary English. It's also a simple guide to the wide world of publishing. It's not an in-depth how-to book about any particular niche of writing, although many niches are mentioned. Suppose you have a special interest in fiction, biography, memoir, stage plays, or screenplays. In that case, there are plenty of full-immersion instruction manuals on the market—and plenty of online tutorials and in-person classes you can attend.

If you are far enough along in your career to tackle a niche project, some of this book may be too basic for you. On the other hand, it may help you with some of the most fundamental issues facing writers at all levels. "Back to the basics" is usually a good plan for every endeavor.

Intended to be read chapter-by-chapter, it can be read at random, too. Everything begins with words on paper.

— *Barry M. Willis*

Sonoma County, California

2025

Chapter 1

WRITE FOR THE EAR, NOT FOR THE EYE

Human language is an auditory phenomenon. It developed over hundreds of thousands of years to be spoken, sung, whispered, and shouted. Its hundreds of varieties can convey an astounding array of information, observations, and emotions—all through the deceptively simple process of hearing.

Spoken language predated its visual depiction by many millennia, but in the modern era of nearly universal literacy in many (but not all) parts of the globe, we have been taught to write for the eye, not for the ear. Graphic designers and speed-reading teachers may think otherwise, but it goes against the thrust of evolution.

At its core, language will always be auditory. Writers who fail to grasp this are doomed to produce reams of impenetrable, pointless prose that is far more effective at inducing lethargy than anything the pharmaceutical industry has ever developed.

Bookstores and the internet are full of such stuff—books that you toss aside after the first two chapters, online articles that don't hold your interest sufficiently for you to click over to the next page.

And these are works that have survived the editorial gauntlet and have made it into print. Imagine those that got rejected!

It doesn't have to be so.

First bit of advice for aspiring writers: listen to music. Listen to any kind of music. Listen to music you like and maybe some that you don't. Music activates the brain in ways no other art form can replicate. It connects directly to your emotions, provokes memories, and forges associations that you can't recreate any other way.

Second bit of advice: Listen to fire-and-brimstone Gospel preachers. Many have a genius for connecting with and arousing their congregations. Listen to the easy introduction, the assertions, the warnings, the admonitions, the repeated refrain, the rising and falling rhythm, the call-and-response, the thundering conclusion.

There's no better training for writers than paying close attention to such verbal artists. They are experts at delivering their message.

Third bit of advice: read extensively and critically. This doesn't mean indiscriminately. It means sample widely. What hooks you, and what doesn't? What resonates for you and what leaves you wishing you were organizing your sock drawer instead?

Final bit of advice: write about what you know. This was supposedly Mark Twain's sage comment to the young Jack London. Better still: write about your passions. You'll have a lot more fun and be far more successful writing about a field of deep interest than you will picking a topic at random—or being assigned a topic at random by an overworked editor or corporate boss.

Listen to your own voice. Develop your own voice. Make your work sing on the page, and you will elevate yourself above the hordes of wooden-eared writers.

Editors will thank you.

Chapter 2

SO, YOU WANT TO BE A WRITER

What do you want to write about? How do you want to write it?

Those may seem like simple questions, but they are fundamental to your projects. Do you want to tell the story of how your great-great-great-grandmother crossed the prairie in a covered wagon?

Or do you want to write about how a neighbor made a fortune as an inventor in his basement?

Maybe you're a fan of "romantasy", or female-centric, lightweight erotica. Also known as "bodice rippers," this genre is a publishing evergreen—one that's always popular. If you can generate a few hundred words per day on Lord Mountebank's insistent manhood and Lady Ashbrooke's heaving bosom, you can make a decent living without leaving the comforts of home.

Everything in the vast universe has potential for observation and elucidation—yes, *everything*. All of it can be written about entertainingly and informatively—or tediously and boringly. The difference is all in how you choose to tell your tale.

Many beginning writers struggle to find a voice. They may feel that their work lacks substance or feels inauthentic. The solution to this is simple: write more and read voraciously. Imitate writers whose work you admire, without plagiarizing. Your authentic voice—or several voices—will emerge from all the imitation.

Many singers learn their craft by performing with recordings. They sing along with their favorites until they feel confident enough to sing on their own. This was the route taken by 16-year-old Danielle Bradbery, a winner of the popular NBC talent show *The Voice*. A small-town girl who had never performed in public before auditioning for the show, Bradbery perfected her technique singing in her bedroom, using a hairbrush as a make-believe microphone. Her passion and persistence landed her not only a first-place win but a recording contract with a major label.

Chances are that you're not going to be offered a staff position at *The New Yorker* with the publication of your first piece, but getting anything published anywhere for the first time—especially if you're also getting paid—is incredibly exhilarating validation and proof that you're on the right path. Once you've got that first one under your belt, follow it immediately with another. Editors love reliable, consistent writers.

Many aspiring writers feel that they need credentials—a master's degree in English Literature at minimum, or summer vacations spent at writers' retreats. The counterargument is that many successful and well-regarded writers have no formal training and/or have pursued fields of study far removed from literature. There's a corresponding belief among some that the publishing world is some sort of pyramid with small-circulation literary quarterlies at the bottom and intellectual juggernauts like *The Atlantic* and *The Economist* at the top.

The fact is that publications of all kinds—periodicals and websites—are hungry monsters that must be fed continually. They are like old-fashioned steam locomotives that need constant stoking with coal to keep moving. Despite the received wisdom that print is dead, a visit to any bookstore will prove the opposite. There are more print publications in production now than ever before, and they all need material.

Inquiries to publishers aren't likely to yield results, but penetrating the apparent barrier may be as simple as sending in a piece unbidden to someone at the upper end of an editorial department. Pieces that arrive fully developed—concise, solidly structured, competently edited, and ready to publish—are like gifts from heaven to overworked editors.

The purpose of *Foundation* is to help you develop your work, whatever form it may take, into compelling pieces that will gain you a following among readers and editors alike.

Chapter 3

KNOW WHERE
YOU'RE GOING

Screenwriting guru Syd Field worked for many years as a script reader for major film studios. Each morning, he would face a stack of scripts to read and pass up the development chain or reject as unusable.

Hundreds of scripts—each one a potential feature film—passed through his hands. He came to the realization that if he wasn't hooked a few pages in, the script wasn't worth pursuing. And he saw a pattern in the ones he rejected and the ones he recommended. What he learned on the job became the basis of his famous "plot point" theory, put forth in his book *Screenplay*, and the foundation of his seminars on successful scriptwriting. He told his students:

> *If you want to drive from San Francisco to Seattle, you look at a map and plan a route. San Francisco is your starting point, and Seattle is your destination. There are infinite numbers of ways to go from one to the other, but having a definite start and stop gives your*

trip a structure. Without it, you're just driving around aimlessly.

Driving around aimlessly is a great metaphor for most amateur writing—blogs, journals, social media posts, internet musings. Much such writing lacks structure and the motive force of a strong opening and a definite conclusion.

You've got to know where you're going. This may mean writing your ending first, even if it's just your closing sentence. That gives you a goal to work toward. Then write your opening. Now you can do whatever you want between these two bookends, because you have a structure to work within.

Whether it's a 30-second commercial, a 30-minute sitcom, a three-hour opera, a 500-word op-ed, or a 1000-page work of historical fiction, every compelling story has, at its core, a three-act structure. Exposition-development-resolution: these are the creative tripod on which your work depends. Secondary to these—but not by much—are premise, point-of-view, and narrative style. Understanding the importance of each and how they work together is essential to honing your craft as a professional writer.

Some writers have an innate organic understanding of these elements, but any intelligent person can develop it through active reading, watching, and listening, even during lazy recreational periods. Don't simply veg out with a favorite TV show. Analyze why you like it. What's the setup, the conflict, the resolution? Are the characters appealing or despicable? Does their interaction make sense? Is their dialog believable? Is their situation realistic? Why is the story funny or sad?

You can apply these analytical tools to every bit of media that comes your way. Doing so will make you less tolerant of fuzzy logic and sloppy writing and much more eager to communicate on a higher level—both intellectually and emotionally. The trip you take your readers on will be a lot more fulfilling than merely driving around aimlessly, despite the fun it may seem to offer while you're doing it.

Syd Field's experience as a script reader also points to another massive truth about successful writing: you've got to hook 'em up front. Scripts without strong openings or premises got tossed aside, just as you would return a potential purchase to the shelf while browsing in a bookstore.

As an example: "When they think of huge openings, people often think of me." So says Hedwig, the transsexual East German rock star in John Cameron Mitchell's wonderful redemption story *Hedwig and the Angry Inch*.

Hedwig's laconic self-deprecation is a joke, of course, but at the joke's core is wise advice: Go big. Open strong. Establish your territory. Take command of your audience.

Every successful form of entertainment has a powerful opening and a strong stance.

In *Hedwig and the Angry Inch*, it's the band's performance before an uncomprehending audience in a scuzzy salad bar called Bilgewater's. In Herman Melville's timeless novel *Moby Dick*, it's the narrator's introduction: "Call me Ishmael." In Leonard Gardner's *Fat City*, it's a bare description of the squalid quarters where the aspiring boxer Billy Tully resides: "He lived in the Hotel Coma." The hotel's name encompasses the essence of the Sacramento Valley town of Stockton, California, in the late 1950s.

A strong lead is an incredibly powerful hook for capturing readers. If you've got them up front, you've probably got them all the way to the end. But that strong opening must take your readers into an equally compelling narrative landscape.

Tell me your tale. Arguably among the greatest country songs ever penned, Merle Haggard's "Mama Tried" is a paragon of simple narrative strength, unfolding a personal tragedy in elegant stanzas like these:

> *The first thing I remember knowing*
> *Was a lonesome whistle blowing*
> *And a young'un's dream of growing up to ride*
> *On a freight train leaving town*
> *Not knowing where I'm bound*
>
> *No one could change my mind, but Mama tried*
>
> *One and only rebel child*
> *From a family meek and mild*
> *My mama seemed to know what lay in store*
> *Despite all my Sunday learning*
> *Towards the bad I kept on turning*
> *Till Mama couldn't hold me anymore*
>
> *And I turned twenty-one in prison doing life*
> *without parole*
> *No one could steer me right, but Mama tried,*
> *Mama tried*
> *Mama tried to raise me better,*
> *but her pleading I denied*
> *That leaves only me to blame 'cause Mama tried*

A great many would-be writers could—*should*—study this song to discover how much power lies in lyrical simplicity. In this case: longing, foreshadowing, foreboding, loneliness, rebellion, crime, guilt, consequences, regret, and ultimately, self-acceptance—all while honoring the parent whose loving guidance was long ignored.

The tale couldn't be told any better or with any more insight by any novelist, regardless of stature. It's consistently strong from beginning to end.

Your work should be too.

Chapter 4

PRESS RELEASES: SOMETIMES LESS IS MORE

As an aspiring writer, you probably have a "day job," perhaps working for a small company whose few employees perform multiple tasks that in larger firms are handled by specialists. Be careful about sharing your writing talents with your colleagues and management, because sooner or later, you'll be recruited to handle internal communications, press relations, website content, and perhaps even advertising.

This will probably be in addition to your heavy workload.

You may be flattered by the attention. Once you volunteer to take on any of these responsibilities, you may discover that supervisors and managers who couldn't write a coherent, simple sentence if their lives depended on it will be altering and editing your work, and making suggestions about how it should read, or demanding endless revisions of pieces that are already as good as they will ever get.

This is why Microsoft Word comes equipped with a "Track Changes" feature, so that everyone in the information chain has an opportunity to change "glad" to "happy" and back again.

Many companies hire outside consultants to produce their websites and printed literature. Contract workers may churn out verbiage by the yard because no one in the communications chain knows how to do it clearly and concisely. Thus, we have the syndrome of the internet: a short-attention-span medium with no practical length limit, where would-be writers can go on forever.

In the internet age, many aspiring writers haven't logged time with print publications where every feature has a length limit—say, 500 words for a movie review or 1,500 words for an in-depth story. This kind of training is invaluable because it teaches you to say everything pertinent within a confined structure.

Often, people hired to write about products and services have no real knowledge of the subjects they're writing about and pad their text with industry jargon to make it sound authoritative. They write at length because they believe that's what the client wants, and they're often right. Clients may congratulate themselves for having purchased sheer volume, without understanding that a few choice words deliver the message while a barrage blunts it.

You may be called upon to go down the rabbit hole of public relations. Many PR novices think that it's a big opportunity to show off their mastery of the writing craft and will produce multi-page documents without understanding either the subject of their writing or the audience for whom it's intended: journalists, people in related industries, or possibly retail customers. Lengthy press releases often hype some new variant on an existing technology as a "solution" and are peppered with undefined acronyms, as anyone who has received Silicon Valley announcements can attest.

Reality? A good press release says everything it needs to say on one page. Everything in it is clear and well-defined, and it is crafted so that journalists can copy its essentials into a news story. Short ones get noticed and used—the word goes out, as intended—while lengthy ones get discarded.

Keep it honest and straightforward. Resist the temptation to call your six-month-old startup "a leading supplier of global solutions" because all your competitors do so. Find a way to make your statement as unambiguous as possible. This is business writing, not literary fiction.

General Motors CEO Mary T. Barra is a great example. A careerist who worked her way up the ranks at the automaker, she's renowned for clearing away conceptual detritus. When she ran GM's human relations department, she reduced the company's densely written dress code to this: "Dress appropriately."

Less is more.

Pundits as varied as architect Mies van der Rohe and former president Jimmy Carter have uttered variations on this universal truth. Nowhere is it more applicable than in public relations and advertising.

Perhaps the best-ever example was a Nikon campaign. Rather than bleating on *ad infinitum* about the technology behind the company's new flagship, the ad copy was instead a simple, beautiful photo of the new camera with this four-word message: "Imported from the Future."

Chapter 5

A MOMENT IN TIME

E very era has its linguistic fads. Ours is prone to borrowings from engineering and technology, or at the very least borrowings that sound technical, efficient, precise, and authoritative—even if they don't mean much or are blatant nonsense.

Foremost among these is "a moment in time," repeated by pundits, politicians, business people, and newscasters in the belief that its inclusion adds gravitas and urgency to their pronouncements: "Tom, I'm standing here at City Hall, where at this moment in time protesters are gathering."

We hear this sort of small-scale pomposity all the time and seldom stop to consider how stupid it is. We already have the perfectly serviceable English word "now," which, when inserted into the statement above, renders it "Tom, I'm standing here at City Hall, where protestors are now gathering." But even using "now" is superfluous, because it's implied in present-tense phrases "I'm standing" and "are gathering." If protesters are gathering, they are doing it now—obviously. At this moment in time.

Another popular phrase repeated by the same offenders is "going forward," a bit of pseudo-official jargon that means simply "in the future," but with the implication of having pondered all possibilities and of having recognized and corrected past wrongs. If an executive announces a change in production, such as discontinuing a once-popular model, she may say, "Going forward, we will no longer offer the Mercury Manatee," rather than "As of September, we will discontinue the Manatee." Both "going forward" and "in the future" are implied in the future-tense verb "will discontinue." No further modifications needed.

Particularly annoying is the hijacking of "optics"—a real technical term referring to the behavior of light—as a substitute for "appearances," as in "The president's deferrals to the dictator were 'bad optics.'" Add to this the business world's fascination with "pivot" as code for "change." Then there's the ad-writer's gimmick of making any noun into a verb by adding the preposition "to," as in "a better way to brain." Really?

Dozens of examples will leap out at you once you start to pay attention. You'll begin to get a handle on how to write for business clients—and how not to write for a literate audience.

The English language is constantly being distorted by people seeking promotional advantage, trying to rise above the noise with clever turns of phrase—phrases that often spread like grass fires and die out almost as quickly. Remember "he's got my back" as a compliment to a trusted colleague?

Trendy jargon may make a corporate client comfortable, but using it elsewhere will put a time-stamp on your work as surely as avocado-colored appliances make a kitchen scream "1970s."

English is full of clichés, many from the Bible and Shakespeare. Phrases such as "a moment in time" and "he's got my back" are recently minted. They sounded fresh and significant when they first hit the word market, but quickly lost value.

Your writing will be instantly elevated if you swear never to use "first and foremost," "last but not least," "a method to his madness," "a way with words," "let's lean into (or unpack) that," "between a rock and a hard place," and any of the many dozens of easy-default sayings that get tossed around in casual conversation. They are fine for informal discussions, but as written elements, they lack imagination.

You're better than that.

Another common glitch is interchanging "in to" with "into"—a mistake all too easy to make and one all too easy for proofreaders and editors to miss. Here's a snippet of a news report about a pending case in the U.S. Supreme Court. We won't name the guilty party, but it's one who most definitely should have known better: "...it comes as the former president is still bitter that the Supreme Court did not step into reverse election results..."

Do you see what's wrong? As written, "reverse election results" becomes a noun phrase, like "a mound of cattle manure," that the Supreme Court avoids stepping in. What the heck are "reverse results?" All would be fine had the writer simply hit the space bar so that SCOTUS "did not step in to reverse election results." This way, "to reverse" is a properly rendered infinitive, acting on "election results."

Problem solved.

This same news report also includes the following: "In court papers, they make clear that the case is forward-looking, not meant to impact the last election but future challenges going forward."

Wow! "Forward-looking," "future challenges," and "going forward"—all in one sentence.

How much redundancy can one sentence bear? "Future challenges" are by definition "going forward," and a case examining ramifications for future elections is by definition "forward-looking." This offending string of verbiage should have been chopped to: "... the case applies only to future challenges, not the last election."

As has been said in many other contexts, "As simple as possible, but no simpler."

And that leads us to the world of anachronisms.

Roman centurions wearing sunglasses. Civil War soldiers with cell phones. These are examples of anachronisms, things not of their time. Some people are sensitive to such assaults on logic, while others never notice.

It's an issue tangentially related to trendy jargon. People tend to believe that if something exists, it must have always existed. That's easy to understand from the perspective of the very young. Twenty-year-olds may assume that big flat-panel TVs and laptop computers have always existed because, for them, they always have.

A similar assumption applies to standard phrases, often used by writers who either don't know any better or do so because their use makes historical fiction seem more vivid. In the otherwise true-to-the-era HBO series *Masters of Sex,* there's a scene where human sexuality researchers Masters and Johnson are poring over files of potential subjects for their study. Johnson hands a folder to Dr. Masters, with a comment like "This one looks promising." Dr. Masters replies, "He's a nonstarter."

What's wrong here? *Masters of Sex* is set in the early 1950s. The term "nonstarter" didn't enter the popular lexicon until decades later. It simply was not used in 1953.

Writers at all levels have contemporized works of historical fiction. Even Shakespeare did it. In Act 2, Scene 2 of *Julius Caesar,* Brutus says, "Caesar, the clock has struck eight."

Think about this. Mechanical clocks were commonplace in Shakespeare's time, but did not exist in ancient Rome. The Romans used sundials and water clocks. Shakespeare may or may not have known that, but he threw in this line for dramatic effect. His audience would certainly not have known nor cared.

Astute readers do care and may not take you seriously if you include too many anachronisms. Minor ones may pass unnoticed, but egregious ones will get you labeled as a hack. A fascinating corollary is the attempt to contemporize historical documents to make them more accessible to modern readers—a new translation of the Bible or the Magna Carta, for example.

In mid-July 2025, National Public Radio featured a fascinating profile of translator Mary Jo Bang's two-decade-long effort to render Dante Alighieri's enduring trilogy, *Inferno*, *Purgatorio*, and *Paradiso*, into modern language, including pop culture references. How she funded the project and how she sustained the drive to complete it were not covered in the interview. Still, her achievement is a fascinating example of viewing the past through a contemporary lens.

Chapter 6

"ME AND MY BUDDIES WENT FISHING"

There are many common expressions and grammatical constructions that are acceptable in casual conversation but should never be used in formal writing—except, perhaps, as dialogue.

"Me and my buddies went fishing," "Me and Jen are at the mall"—common sentences in everyday English, but they're glaringly ungrammatical. "Me" is the objective first-person singular pronoun, meaning that it signifies the receiver of an action rather than the initiator: "The truck hit me."

Should you ever doubt this, simply drop "and my buddies," and see what's left: "Me went fishing." This sounds like something a toddler might say, but people do it all the time because they feel that a properly constructed sentence—"My buddies and I went fishing"—sounds pretentious.

It could be argued that the phrase "me and my buddies" is a collective noun and is therefore acceptable as the subject of a sentence, but it's not an argument that will sway many grammarians. Subjective pronouns are always and forever, *I, you, he, she, it, we, you,* and *they.* There are no alternatives.

A fascinating reversal of this linguistic oddity is the common construction "for you and I." Many people—even those with advanced degrees—use variations of this in conversation: "between you and I," "for she and he." They do this because they think it sounds more proper than "for you and me," but it's dead wrong.

Songwriters sometimes know better but default to bad grammar as it gives them more options for rhymes, but the fact is that pronouns in the objective case (receivers of action) are always and forever: *me, you, him, her, it, us you,* and *them.* Should you doubt this, again simply drop the "and" construction and see what's left: "It's a wonderful opportunity for you and I" becomes "a wonderful opportunity for I." Sheer illiterate nonsense.

A third common error—one that's harder to identify—is agreement of subject and verb in complex sentences. You may hear a newscaster say something like "A team of researchers believe that they may have found a cure for facial tics."

What's wrong here? Collective nouns such as *team* and *company* take singular verbs in American English. This news should be appropriately rendered as "A team of researchers believes..." because "team", not "researchers," is the subject of the sentence; "of researchers" is a prepositional phrase modifying "team." People often make this mistake because "researchers" (plural) occurs next to the verb. Such gaffes may go unnoticed in everyday conversation, but they are amateurish mistakes in writing, among the most frequent corrections that copy editors have to make.

Interestingly, in British English, collective nouns take third person verbs. "The team are coming onto the pitch" is proper British, while "The team *is* coming onto the field" is proper American.

More: Like rodents getting into seemingly impenetrable buildings, colloquialisms have a way of sneaking into many pieces of otherwise respectable writing. Among the most common is the phrase "try and..." as in "Try and start the car." or "Try and win the game."

Any middle-school English teacher would become justifiably livid at these sentences, which should be correctly rendered as "Try to start the car.", and "Try to win the game."

Commonly used throughout the English-speaking world, in both written and spoken communication, "try and" is a hard habit to break, primarily because it occupies a bit of a gray area. The addition of a comma, as in "Try, and win the game" makes the sentence perfectly grammatical. Inserting a period (or "full stop") does something similar, as in "Try. Start the car."

These gray-area examples are statistical outliers—the phrase "try and" is almost entirely used in place of "try to," and so often that editors often don't notice, or more likely, don't consider it important enough to change. That's a pity, because "try to" is still the proper expression.

Try. Avoid writing "try and."

Chapter 7

I MEAN, THAT'S VERY UNIQUE

Most people have some vague familiarity with the scientific concept of "absolute zero"—a temperature so low that it can't possibly get any colder. That's why it's called absolute.

The English language has a handful of absolute adjectives: they describe qualities or conditions that can't be exceeded. *Unique* is foremost among them—a word that means "singular, unlike any other." The addition of adverbs can't reinforce such absolute adjectives, because they are already at the peak of descriptiveness.

There's neither room for nor need to bulk them up, and in fact, trying to do so only weakens them.

You may hear an *America's Got Talent* judge say something like, "That was a very unique performance." It's probably an attempt to shower praise, but the addition of *very*—an adverb known among grammarians as an intensifier—degrades the intended praise by making it sound like something a high-schooler would say. The only effective way to say this is "That was a unique performance."

Like gas tanks filled to their limits, absolutes can't be added to, but they can be subtracted from. You can say "That was an almost unique performance," acknowledging the mostly original nature of the performance while implying that some of it was cribbed from others—an efficient, elegant, and diplomatic bit of criticism. And depending on the tone with which it's delivered, "That was a unique performance" could be high praise or scathing dismissal, meaning "That was the worst thing I have ever seen"—a distinction easy to make with tone of voice and damned difficult to convey in writing.

No respectable art critic would ever describe a painting as "very stunning"—as with "unique," the addition of "very" weakens "stunning" rather than making it more profound. But she might qualify her appraisal this way: "Visually stunning, the painting is conceptually disturbing..." By doing so, she modifies the absolute without diminishing its power. Likewise, the *America's Got Talent* judge could say, "That was a vocally unique performance, but the choreography was lifted from *Rent*."

In skilled hands, descriptive adverbs can enhance the meaning of absolutes, but intensifiers can only detract.

Interestingly, the first line of the preamble to the U.S. Constitution contains an ungrammatical attempt to gussy up an absolute: "...in order to form a more perfect union..." *Perfect* describes an absolute quality; if something is perfect, it can't be made more perfect.

The Founding Fathers were hedging their bets with that one.

The "very unique" construction seems to be common among people who begin responses to questions with the phrase "Yeah. I mean..." It's unknown where this linguistic fad originated, but it's popular among millennials. You may hear a young athlete being interviewed after a game, saying to reporters, "Yeah. I mean, our defense did a fantastic job..."

Traditionally, "I mean" is a lead-in to clarify some previous statement, as in "We had a rough time out there but came through in the end. I mean, our defense did a fantastic job."

As is frequently the case, "I mean" implies that the responder has considered a response but has not spoken it. He or she comes off sounding like someone interrupted while daydreaming—an example of reluctance to make a strong, definite statement. It's reluctance that aspiring writers should never exhibit.

Chapter 8

PAST HISTORY AND FUTURE PLANS

"That's past history. What's your future plan?"

These two sentences were actually uttered back-to-back by a respected newscaster conducting an interview. Both sentences are screaming examples of redundancy—the repetition of ideas, sometimes done intentionally for effect, but often spoken or written in ignorance. It's a much-needed recurring topic in *Foundation*.

"Past history" and "future plan" are both redundant because history is about the past—there isn't really any other kind, and a plan is always about the future. You can't plan for the past or present. You can plan short-term or long-term, but planning is always about making something happen at a time some distance away: plans for next Tuesday and for your retirement 30 years hence are all about the future.

English is full of redundancies—so full that we seldom stop to consider how ridiculous and needless they are. "Revert back" is a popular one. There's no need for "back" because "revert" means literally "to go back." A football coach may explain his team's uneven performance by saying, "We had to revert back to our running game after our quarterback was injured." He might more properly say "We had to revert to our running game..." or "We had to go back..." but he likely believes "revert back" is correct because he's heard it all his life.

In a *CNN* broadcast, media analyst Brian Stelter said, "Tucker Carlson had 24 hours of advance notice..." about the resignation of *Fox News* writer Blake Neff. "Notice" is always in advance to some degree; Stelter might more appropriately have said "Carlson had 24 hours' notice..."

The same holds for any similar word—"advance warning" is equally redundant. All warnings are in advance. If they weren't, they wouldn't be warnings. Such words can be modified by explanatory text, however: "Due to a power outage, the delayed warning came too late to be of any use." Note that "early warning" and "late warning" are both correct, but "advance warning" is not.

Next, how about this from an emergency dispatcher: "Where is your location at?"—a five-word question of which three reference the caller's whereabouts: *where, location,* and *at.* Only one is needed: "Where are you?" or perhaps "What's your location?"

Fox News commentator Greg Gutfeld has a habit of plying redundancies. "Directionally, where are we going?" pops up sometimes from him. He's trying to sound intellectual, but instead bluffs like a high school freshman stalling for time. "Directionally" and "where" both refer to the same thing. It's like saying, "We saw it optically." Other than "seeing it in your mind's eye," optics are the only way we see.

You usually can't go wrong by keeping it simple.

But redundancy isn't always bad. Sometimes it can be hilarious. A highly educated former girlfriend of mine spouted this as we passed a gym still packed at a late hour: "Look! All those great big, huge, gigantic workout guys!"—a glorious string of adjectives describing enormity. Her vocabulary had momentarily defaulted to childhood level when she couldn't come up with "bodybuilders."

All of this passes in casual conversation, and it's often entertaining, but beware of it sneaking into your writing. You may be tempted to describe some springtime pasture as "...a lush green verdant meadow...", without understanding that *verdant* means lush and green. As a descriptor, verdant is so lush that adding to it is actually a detraction. Let your verdant meadow stand alone.

Chapter 9

THE DECEPTIVE ALLURE OF SPELL-CHECKING

*F*eet and *feat:* English is riddled with *homophones*, words that are pronounced alike but are spelled differently and have different meanings.

In this case, your pedal extremities and an achievement—two concepts so wildly divergent that it would be difficult to mistake one for the other—unless you are relying on your word processor's spell-check function to make sure you have used the right one. "The dog did an amazing feat" and "The dog had amazing feet" are as different from each other as they can be, but sound alike when spoken. (The French word *fête,* a celebration, is actually pronounced *feht,* unless you grew up in the American Midwest, where proper pronunciation of foreign words is considered pretentious.)

There are many others: *we* and *wee, know* and *no, do* and *dew, so* and *sew*—and the perpetually misconstrued *they're, their,* and *there.*

English is not the only language with homophones. The French word *tour* has two distinct meanings—one, a meandering journey, as in *Le Tour de France,* and the other, a tall structure, as in *La Tour Eiffel,* the Eiffel Tower. The Russian word *pol* can mean "half," "floor," or "sex," depending on context, and is understood organically by native speakers.

Because English is a blend of languages, it offers an enormous vocabulary and a fantastic opportunity for nuance. These benefits bring many potential pitfalls that aren't always identified by spell-checking programs.

In spoken language, we gather meaning by context. Spell-checkers have some primitive contextual capabilities but are no substitute for astute human editors.

Blind-faith reliance on spell-checkers can yield comical results, especially when combined with voice-recognition writing programs. This headline actually scrolled across the screen during a *CNN* news broadcast: "HHS Launching Testing Sites in COVID-19 Hots Pots," and this one appeared in a *Marin Independent Journal* news story about the importance of fire prevention: "Hire fire danger in coming months." Humans were asleep at the wheel in both cases.

Spell-checkers can miss transposed letters in similar words: "post" and "pots" may not be flagged as wrong, even if they are. Be sure that you want "tip" instead of "top"—"The tip of the iceberg" and "The top of the iceberg" are not interchangeable.

And be sure that the homophone you select is the proper one. The words *right, rite, write,* and *wright* may all pass unnoticed by your spell-checker, even though the misuse of any will leap out at an editor. Computers have made the writer's life easier in many ways, but there's still no substitute for a keen eye and an alert mind.

The vagaries of English spelling can be persistent problems even for the most experienced writers. Why does *bough* rhyme with *now*, but *rough* and *tough* rhyme with *buff*?

Why does *through* rhyme with *grew*, but *thorough* rhymes with *burrow* and *burro*? Why does *cat* begin with *c* but *kitten* with a *k*? Why does *quick* have three different letters for the *k* sound, and why is one of them silent?

Why does *feline* begin with *f*, but *pharmacy* with *ph*? Why is the verb *pronounce* but the noun is *pronunciation*? What is the point of double consonants, as in *little, commitment*, and *millennial*? Wouldn't one be sufficient?

Then we have the issue of functional names: why do *hunter* and *carpenter* end in *er*, while *conductor* and *donor* end in *or*? Why is *x* pronounced *eks* in the middle of a word but *z* if it's the lead letter, as in *xylophone* and *Xavier*—a name correctly pronounced *Zavier*, not *Ex-zavier*?

How about words that end in *le* or *el*—mantel and *title*, for example? Why aren't they all spelled alike? Is there any logic to that? Probably no more than in the crazy-making use of *ie and ei* in words such as *chief* and *deceive*.

Welcome to the *Looney Tunes* world of English spelling and the almost-as-crazy world of English pronunciation. Why is *schedule* pronounced *sked-ual* in America but *shed-ual* in much of the United Kingdom?

Because English was derived from multiple languages, there are many conceivable ways that anything can be spelled. Despite the saintly patience of English teachers who did their best to teach us spelling rules, the fact is that the only way to be a good speller is to memorize every word, one by one.

Chapter 10

THE MISUNDERSTOOD APOSTROPHE

A neighbor down the hill from where I live has a hand-scrawled cardboard sign in his yard: "Buoy's for Sale."

I'm reasonably sure he means "Buoys for Sale," as he has several on display, but with a misplaced apostrophe, his sign literally reads "Buoy <u>is</u> for sale." That is not his intention, of course. What he's done with his signage is among the most common mistakes in English, but he's retired now, so I'm not sure it troubles him.

In any event, pity the poor apostrophe, our language's most abused and misunderstood punctuation mark.

It's used to denote two things: first, possession, as in *Anna's car*, and second, a missing word or piece of information, as in the contraction *don't* (do not). It's also used, inexplicably, by some publications to indicate the plural of acronyms, as in *CD's* and *DVD's*, inducing all kinds of confusion in people who then assume, like my neighbor with buoys for sale, that an apostrophe indicates a plural.

It does not. *CDs and DVDs* would be far more logical, but try telling that to any old-school editor at an East Coast newspaper.

A corollary to the misused apostrophe is the widespread melding of *it's* (it is) with *its*, a possessive adjective like *my, your, his, her, our,* and *their.* The difference: "It's a beautiful day." vs. "The law was far-reaching; its effect was felt nationwide." This should be clear to most folks, but many people—even those with advanced degrees—use them interchangeably or are simply unable to tell the difference.

Sometimes you will even see the abomination *its'*. There is no such construction in English. It is just plain <u>wrong</u>.

A similar situation involves *who's* (who is) and *whose* (the possessive adjective). These two words are pronounced alike but have very different meanings: "Who's on first?" vs. "Whose hat is this?"

Further confusion ensues with names that end in *s*, plurals, and plural possessives, thanks in part to Strunk and White's classic writer's text, *The Elements of Style.* We all agree that "Anna's car" is configured correctly. Still, Strunk and White insist that to be consistent, a different car should be designated "James's car"—a construction that's fallen out of fashion, as have, for some practitioners anyway, repeated (serial or Oxford) commas.

> *(Author's Note: My editor loves Oxford commas, so...*
> *The comma, incidentally, was invented in the Middle*
> *Ages when few people could read. It was a marker for*
> *orators to take a pause.)*

Moving on, we may have been taught that the phrase "The big, brown, aggressive dog..." is proper, but current usage would render it as "The big brown aggressive dog..." and the automobile in question as "James' car"—simpler, cleaner, and easier to read, some say.

Things can get really squirrely when you're confronted with a combination of proper names ending in *s* with plural possession, as in describing a home belonging to "The Williams family". Is it the *Williams* house, the *Williams'* house, the *Williams's* house, or—God save us—the *Williamses'* house?[1]

Only the first two choices offer any hope of modern clarity, and both are correct. In the first, *Williams* is an adjective describing the house, and in the second, with the appended apostrophe, it becomes a possessive adjective. The meaning is clear either way. The final two are archaic and should be avoided. Please.

You may think that obsessing over punctuation is for English Lit geeks only and that it doesn't really matter as long as you are getting your ideas across. No, gentle reader, it is not that simple: if it doesn't <u>really</u> matter, why are you bothering to write at all? You could simply text or tweet in all caps to convey your misspelled points.

But knowledge of and facility with both grammar and punctuation will separate you from countless thousands of functional semi-literates out there. Understanding the nuances of our language will not only elevate your writing but can also be fun.

Don't believe it?

Pick up a copy of *Eats, Shoots & Leaves*, the vastly entertaining riff on punctuation by British editor and grammarian Lynne Truss,

---

1   Fair warning. Some English purists may take umbrage at my definitions in this paragraph. So be it.

founding member of the Apostrophe Police. She doesn't suffer fools gladly and, in a brilliant display of literary glissando, can go from mild annoyance to homicidal rage within one paragraph. (True talent, that.)

According to Truss, "If you consider yourself an educated person and still don't know the difference between *it's* and *its*, you deserve to be chopped into little pieces and fed to the fish."

Harsh? Oh yes, but her book is your indispensable guide as a writer (and, one might posit, as a reader) when you venture into the punctuation wilderness.

Chapter 11

FEAR OF "TO BOLDLY GO" AND OTHER FALSE PHOBIAS

T he *Star Trek* mission statement, "To boldly go where no one has gone before," has been criticized many times by grammarians who insist that it's wrong because inserting the adverb *boldly* between *to* and *go* yields a so-called "split infinitive."

What's an infinitive? It's the absolute version of a verb: that is to say, the ideal or idealized form. Another way to think of an infinitive is that it's the <u>name</u> of a verb.

Legend has it that the split infinitive phobia arose among academics schooled in Latin. The problem with obsessing over split infinitives is that English doesn't have real infinitives the way other languages do—such as the French *marcher* (to walk) or the Spanish *beber* (to drink).

In English, infinitives are formed by preceding the root verb with the preposition *to*, as in *to go, to eat, to talk, to run*, etc. While Captain Kirk of the starship *Enterprise* might have been more correct to state "To go boldly where no one has gone before," it might not have the same dramatic impact. Scriptwriters for *Star Trek* were probably well aware of how they were structuring the captain's bold statement.

Don't worry about splitting infinitives because every native speaker of English splits them all the time. Dealing with a victim of a construction accident, an emergency room physician might say to his patient, "This may hurt. I want to gently remove the nail embedded in your foot." That's the usual way this might be expressed. Were the physician grammar-obsessed, he might say instead, "I want to remove the nail in your foot gently."

The problem with this construction is that the adverb *gently* is some distance from *remove*, the verb it's intended to modify. It also sounds a tad stilted. A good rule of thumb is not to worry much about splitting infinitives, but to try to keep the intervening verbiage as short as possible. "To boldly go" will fly, but "To energetically and with great determination go where no one has gone before" probably won't.

Old-school grammarians are also adamant that a properly constructed English sentence should never end with a preposition. By their standards, "That's something I never heard of" is wrong, and "That's something of which I never heard" is correct.

Which sounds right to you?

What do people usually say? The rule against ending sentences with prepositions flies in the face of standard English usage. In fact, this prohibition is belied by most of our ordinary imperatives: *go in*, *go out*, *drive by*, and *come over*.

Ultimately, the only factor that determines what is correct is common acceptance. Trust your ears. You're writing for an audience of intelligent readers. They will find nothing wrong with "That's something I'd like to learn more about."

Chapter 12

PASSIVE AGGRESSION

"The Giants beat the Dodgers with a ninth-inning grand slam that put them up 9-8."

"The game was decided by a ninth-inning grand slam hit by Jose Colinda, resulting in a 9-8 victory for the Giants over the Dodgers."

Which of these two sentences has the more dramatic impact? Which one makes you want to keep reading? Both are perfectly grammatical, and they convey the same information, but the first one grabs our attention because it's in the active voice.

The second one is soporific at best. In passive voice, it tells its tale the slow way, by reciting which action was done by which actor—in this case, two passive phrases stacked one atop the other: "game was decided" and "hit by Colinda."

Passive-voice writing is regrettably common in English, often the default style in research papers, academic treatises, and legal work. The reason for its popularity in those areas is that authors hope the accumulated evidence will lead readers to the desired conclusion without much prodding. They hope that their evidence speaks for itself without the need for strong assertions.

Authors employing the passive voice do so because they wish to appear impartial—even though that is rarely the case—and don't want to use sheer force to try to elevate opinion or supposition to fact. While they may succeed in disguising their own biases, they do so by imposing a tiresome burden on readers.

Lengthy pieces in passive voice are dreadfully dull to read, unless you happen to be a fanatic about the topic at hand. Suppose you are deeply fascinated by World War II, for example. In that case, you may be willing to endure hundreds of pages filled with sentences such as:

> *"The Rhine was crossed by Zhukov and his army, rolling inexorably toward Berlin and the imminent defeat of the Nazis."*

This sentence is really about the action of Zhukov's army, and not about the Rhine, so it should be structured thus:

> *"Zhukov and his army crossed the Rhine and rolled inexorably toward Berlin."*

It's also become trendy among historians, when speaking, to discuss the past in the present tense, as a way of making it more vivid:

> *"Zhukov and his army cross the Rhine and roll toward Berlin."*

They do this verbally to generate excitement, but often go to the passive past tense in written analyses:

> *"Lincoln's fatal wounds were inflicted by assassin John Wilkes Booth."*

Sometimes the passive voice is the only way to express an event or relationship adequately, but it's the literary equivalent of a musty gray blanket. Your readers could quickly lose interest. Resist temptation and use it sparingly.

Lucidly written accounts can be just as vivid as verbal ones. The active voice is what makes them compelling.

Chapter 13

THE PURPOSE OF PARAGRAPHS

Have you ever tried to read one of those lengthy disclaimers that you have to agree to before you can sign up for a new website or download some software?

How about dense legalese or the warnings in microscopic font that accompany prescription drugs? Or a textbook with hundreds of footnotes in a tiny font written by a professor and included as required course reading?

You may have noticed that such materials can be tough sledding because the text isn't broken up into paragraphs—or more likely, not enough paragraphs to make it an easy read.

Why do we need paragraphs? After all, any string of words should read the same regardless of arrangement, yes?

No.

Everything about how words are displayed affects the reader's experience. This is why book designers and graphic artists choose various typefaces for different kinds of projects, and why editors—

good ones, that is—break up lengthy text into smaller, more digestible bites.

The meta-purpose of paragraphs is to impose fewer burdens on readers so that the author's intent is clear.

In the early days of literacy, when only the clergy and a few other educated people could read, text was often written and printed without obvious breaks. This made reading tedious, but the clergy and their secular counterparts had a surplus of time, something in short supply for moderns.

Some writers still engage in this as a sort of artist's experiment. Gabriel García Márquez, one of the world's greatest authors (*One Hundred Years of Solitude* and *Love in the Time of Cholera*), let his self-indulgence get out of control with his *The Autumn of the Patriarch*. The book's first 22 pages are one long run-on sentence without punctuation or paragraph breaks, an impossibility for all but the most fanatical readers. Originally written in Spanish, it must have been a nightmare for its translator. Don't try this. You are not Gabriel García Márquez.

Your well-meaning high school English teacher may have told you that an effectively structured paragraph begins with a "topic sentence," followed by three or four supporting sentences. The next section would start with another topic sentence, with the whole procedure repeated throughout your report or essay.

This was a pleasant conceit and helpful advice for students, but not fully applicable to the craft of writing contemporary prose.

What you really want to do is break up your narrative so that the blank space between sentences serves as a "rest" (in the musical sense) to give your work some rhythm. Mentioned earlier, the comma was invented for a similar purpose, as an indication to oral interpreters where to take a breath.

Appropriate use of paragraphs, commas, and other punctuation marks, and variation in your written delivery, such as long and short sentences and sometimes the dramatic use of sentence fragments, are guarantees that you will reach the broadest possible audience, and that they will remain alert and engaged.

You may not want to simplify your work to the point where it's comprehensible to grade-school kids—unless you're writing children's stories, of course—but you do want to make it as accessible as it can be.

You can't go wrong including as many paragraph breaks as you wish. If they think you went too far with it, your editors will make adjustments.

Your job is to make theirs easier.

Chapter 14

FOUNDATION— DOUBLE NEGATIVES

A ll high school graduates know—or are supposed to know—that in modern English, double negatives are considered at best improper and at worst, indicative of semi-literacy. *I ain't got none* is an ungrammatical response to a question such as "Do you have any money?" Even more ungrammatical are "stacked" negative elements, such as *I don't never have none.*

Centuries ago, the use of double or stacked negatives was commonplace in English, but it fell out of fashion due to the insistence of grammarians trained in logic. Their persuasive argument was that two negative elements canceled each other, so that *I ain't got none* should be interpreted as *I have some.*

Stacked negative elements can be found in documents dating from Shakespeare's time and later, but their use was never widespread in English. A different kind of linguistic logic rules some modern languages, such as Russian, where double and stacked negatives reinforce rather than cancel each other. *Ya nichivo nikogda ni znal* (literally, "I nothing never not knew") translates as "I never knew anything."

Efforts to abandon them in English succeeded. For many generations, teachers have campaigned for clarity on the matter—and, for the most part, have been victorious. We rarely hear or read them, unless they are lines spoken by semi-educated thugs in crime dramas.

Yet double negatives persist in more subtle ways and are used all the time by very well-educated people to express degrees of emotion or acceptance. After having her house painted, a neighbor may comment, "I was not unhappy with the result"—the two negative elements *not* and *un* combining (and mutually canceling, as grammarians insist) to convey that while she wasn't overjoyed, she wasn't disappointed either. "Not unhappy" gets close to the borderline of "happy" while not crossing it.

This subtle double negative technique can be used in multiple ways to express nuances that more straightforward syntax cannot. A sportscaster might humorously describe a massive Sumo wrestler as *not underfed*, a much cleverer description than simply *well fed*.

A political commentator may do something similar with a line such as "The upcoming election is not unlikely to be settled in the courts," indicating a smaller degree of probability than "likely to be settled." And *likely* is only one of many potential adjectives that might be inserted in that statement to raise or lower its stakes: *certain to be settled* is much more definite.

As an aspiring writer, you're probably aware that there are precious few linguistic or grammatical jokes. The double-negative issue is a rarity. In this case, the setup is a first-year linguistics class in which a professor is lecturing on the foregoing topic. "In some languages, such as English," the instructor intones, "Negative elements negate each other. In others, they act as reinforcement, but as far as we know, there are no cases where positive elements negate each other."

To which the class clown responds: "Yeah, right."

Knowing when and how to use such double negatives can add subtlety to your writing. Don't be unwilling to try!

Chapter 15

NARRATIVE FLOW

Awkward sentence structure disrupts narrative flow in every kind of prose, from news reporting to fiction.

Sometimes it's unintentional on the part of harried or wooden-eared writers, and sometimes it's a conscious attempt to adhere to a publication's "house style."

Consider this sentence that appeared in a 2020 *CNN* opinion piece by Joe Lockhart:

> "*Democrats who support Joe Biden will revel in the portrait Cohen, who was Trump's personal attorney, paints of his former client, but they've already made up their mind on voting for Biden.*"

This sentence requires re-reading to determine what exactly Lockhart is trying to say, mainly because of his awkward word and phrase order. It would flow more smoothly this way:

> "*Democrats who support Joe Biden have already made up their minds on voting for him. They will still revel in the unflattering portrait painted of Trump by Cohen, the president's former personal attorney.*"

Two clear, unambiguous sentences convey Lockhart's opinion better than a clumsy one.

Another *CNN* news story from the same day does something similar, this one a bit about a rental truck dumping U.S. Postal Service mail in a parking lot:

> *"U.S. Postal Service employees weren't involved in the dumping of bags, Omar Gonzalez, the western regional coordinator for the American Postal Workers Union, told CNN."*

Why is "told *CNN*" dangling at the end of this sentence?

This bit of info might have been better stated this way:

> *"U.S. Postal Service employees weren't involved in the dumping of bags, according to Omar Gonzalez, Western Regional Coordinator for the American Postal Workers Union,"*

or

> *"Western Regional Coordinator for the American Postal Workers Union Omar Gonzalez told CNN that U.S. Postal Service employees weren't involved in the dumping of bags."*

Compared to the original, there are several more elegant ways to convey this news.

Most egregious in the awkward construction department is *The New Yorker*, queen bee of old-school American literary publications. You won't see awkward construction in any of its superb capsule reviews of plays, movies, restaurants, or art exhibits, because such reviews are written to deliver the maximum amount of information in the shortest possible length—and with maximum entertainment value. Nor will you see it in any of the magazine's one- or two-page humor or opinion pieces, for the same reason.

But awkward construction rears its ugly head in almost every long-form *New Yorker* feature story. A fictitious example:

> " 'Such a soggy day,' Melanie, who was standing at the corner of 51ˢᵗ and Broadway, wearing a yellow slicker and expensive sunglasses, said."

Why are *Melanie*, the subject of the sentence, and *said*, the subject's verb, widely separated by so much intervening prose?

Furthermore, the way this is written implies that the corner of 51ˢᵗ and Broadway is wearing the yellow slicker and expensive sunglasses. This ungainly, arrhythmic approach stops readers in their tracks. Still, it appears in almost every *New Yorker* feature, to such an extent that we can only assume that the magazine's copy editors alter submitted pieces to make them conform to house style.

The description of Melanie might be better expressed thus:

> "In a yellow slicker and expensive sunglasses, Melanie stood at the corner of 51ˢᵗ and Broadway. 'Such a soggy day,' she said."

Simple, clean, logical, and easy to read.

Just because you see a convoluted style repeated in a publication as esteemed as *The New Yorker* doesn't mean that it's right, and it certainly doesn't mean that you should imitate it.

Again: language is an auditory phenomenon. Every sentence takes the reader from here to there. Should you ever doubt the narrative flow of one of your pieces, read it aloud.

Previously unseen road bumps and potholes will leap out at you.

Chapter 16

VERBAL SIBLINGS

Here and there in this book, you'll find what might feel like "remedial lessons," the sort of thing that bored you senseless back in eighth grade. I beg your pardon for the repetition. These are essential tools if you want to write professionally.

English verbs can look simple on the surface, yet they work through tenses and aspects, which combine to convey time, completion, and nuance. The fundamental elements are:

- **Simple:** *I walk. I walked.*
- **Progressive (continuous):** *I am walking. I was walking.*
- **Perfect:** *I have walked. I had walked.*
- **Past progressive:** *I have been walking. I had been walking.*
- **Future progressive:** *I will be walking*

Each aspect expresses something different.

- *I walk across the street every day is a* **simple present** *that implies habit.*

- *I walked across the street yesterday* is **simple past**, *a completed action.*
- *I am walking across the street* is **present progressive**, *an action in progress.*
- *I was walking across the street when the meteor struck* is **past progressive**, *an ongoing action interrupted by another.*

English also has future forms built with **auxiliary verbs**:

- *I will walk across the street.*
- *I will be walking.*
- *I will have been walking for fifty years next week.*

That last one—**future perfect progressive**—shows how precisely English can place an action in time.

Conditional forms add another layer of meaning: *I could walk, I should walk, I would walk.*

Each carries a different implication:

- *could suggests ability or a possibility.*
- *should suggests an obligation.*
- *would suggests a willingness dependent on circumstance: I would walk across the street if the meteor weren't on its way.*

All of these combinations rely on auxiliary verbs, and they allow you to express precisely what you mean—if you use them carefully.

A separate source of confusion comes from English verbs that look related but aren't interchangeable. *Imply* and *infer* are common troublemakers. You *imply* something when you suggest it indirectly: "The president's remarks implied that a strike was imminent." You *infer* something when you draw a conclusion from what was said: "We inferred from his remarks that a strike was imminent."

Another tricky pair: **compose** and **comprise**.

- *100 Senators compose the U.S. Senate describes the parts that create the whole.*

- *The U.S. Senate comprises 100 Senators describes the whole, containing its parts.*

Comprise is the umbrella; *compose* is what's under it.

Fortunately, English doesn't have many of these mismatched verbal siblings—but the few it does have are worth mastering. Consider it an easy and helpful assignment to add these distinctions to your toolbox.

Chapter 17

A POINT OF VIEW
ON POINT OF VIEW

E very piece of writing is founded on a point of view, or a POV in screenwriters' parlance.

A story's point of view may be objective or subjective, from inside or outside depicted events—sometimes called *interiority* and *exteriority* by writing teachers. POV may have a singular perspective or multiple perspectives.

The most common point of view, one that we encounter daily, is the personality-free objective tone of news reporting:

> *An earthquake struck the eastern Mediterranean this morning, collapsing buildings in Greece and Turkey. Several people were killed, and dozens were injured, according to initial announcements from the Greek and Turkish governments.*

This is traditional, straightforward news reporting. A subjective perspective might be a posting from someone who was there:

> *Our tour group had just begun walking through Izmir when we heard a rumble, felt the ground lift, and saw walls cracking and tiles falling from roofs. We heard people screaming in the distance, but didn't know where they were. It was incredibly scary.*

A personal account like this has much more emotional impact than a factual news report. This is why most films focus on a central character's struggle rather than adopting a more distant overview. It's the difference between a compelling drama about one soldier's survival and a documentary about the war itself.

Many novelists attempt an unadorned pseudo-objective style while focusing on a central character. A fictitious example:

> *Sarah hadn't seen Tom in months. She felt pangs of anxiety in anticipation of his visit.*
>
> *There was a knock on the door. She took a deep breath and opened it slowly.*
>
> *"Hello, Sarah," said Tom. "It's good to see you."*
>
> *"Hello, Tom," she replied, and let him in.*

Reporter-turned-novelist Ernest Hemingway pioneered this minimalistic narrative-and-dialogue style, one that has become a default for many American novelists. *This-happened-and-then-that-happened. She-said-this-and-he-said-that.*

If you have a solid plot, you can tell your tale this way, and it will likely find an eager readership. It's not virtuoso writing, to be sure, but it's an accessible style that many readers enjoy.

Point of view is arguably the most essential aspect of the writer's craft—assuming, of course, that you have a handle on grammar, spelling, syntax, and pacing. The same tale can be told in any number of ways. Choosing which way is crucial because it shapes your readers' experience. This is an important lesson for writers to internalize: your story's point of view and narrative style will appeal to some readers but not others.

Ultimately, you need to feel satisfied that your piece conveys what you want it to convey, both informationally and emotionally. If it works for you, after several readings and revisions, it will likely resonate with many readers, too.

Chapter 18

LATER THE SAME POV

T hink about all the stories you have read: in books and magazine articles, online sketches, profiles of personalities, and more. In terms of stories, that's only the <u>written</u> material that has crossed your path. There are also thousands of TV shows and movies that you've seen.

Each began life as a string of words. Those that really stick with you even after you've forgotten who wrote them or where you found them are usually about one character.

That one character has a problem to solve or a mission to accomplish, and if the writing's good, we stay with the story even if—or perhaps, because—it takes us on a journey through unknown territory.

Charles Frazier's *Cold Mountain* debuted in 1997 and topped the *New York Times* best-seller list for sixty-one weeks. It was made into a hit film and spawned an operatic adaptation. That's quite an accomplishment for a story that, at its core, is about a wounded soldier trying to get home at the end of the Civil War.

Margaret Atwood's *The Handmaid's Tale* is a first-person account of a fictional cultural/political takeover by a religious cult of a substantial swath of North America. This enduring story puts a Western spin on a real occurrence—the Islamic Revolution that swept Iran in the late 1970s.

Atwood's vision is all-encompassing, but she shares it through the voice of her narrator, a modern young woman who suddenly finds her world turned upside down and has no way to set it right. Readers may be hooked from the opening paragraphs, not because the premise is so horrific (even though it is), but because they find the narrator's voice and observations so compelling.

Putting your central character in the midst of a real historical upheaval, as Frazier did, or in a fictional-but-plausible one, as Atwood did, or simply in the midst of his or her own confusing circumstances—as J.D. Salinger did with Holden Caulfield in *The Catcher in the Rye*—will give your story solid footing.

It also works for huge, sweeping pieces with dozens of characters, such as Victor Hugo's classic *Les Misérables*, a story that, despite its broad social scope, is essentially about one man, Jean Valjean, imprisoned for stealing bread to feed his family.

The web of class distinction, injustice, poverty, and oppression that defined 19th-century Paris is made stunningly clear through Hugo's focus on a single character. He could have told the story from a broader perspective, as historians would do, but it wouldn't be nearly as compelling. Nor would it have had breakout potential. *Les Misérables* has proven to be not only one of the greatest novels of all time, but an inspiration for massive stage productions and films. Even many people who have never read the book are familiar with Valjean's struggle and the circumstances that gave rise to it. Those who see the film or stage play can identify similar circumstances in the contemporary world, an expansion effect that's still felt far beyond 1862, when the book first appeared.

It's much more challenging to try to give multiple characters equal coverage.

The 1989 film *Shag* is a lightweight romp about four Kennedy-era South Carolina girls who decide to celebrate high school graduation with a weekend in Myrtle Beach, against their parents' wishes.

The premise is a good one, and the depiction of the period is accurate, but the dramatic arc falters as it tries to follow the antics of all four girls over the course of the weekend. Focusing on one while giving the other three adequate comedic exposure would probably have been a more successful strategy and would have rendered a more satisfying story.

Stay focused, but give your secondary characters depth. It's a tricky balancing act, but a very effective one.

Chapter 19

THE IMPORTANCE OF CONFLICT

S hakespeare's *Hamlet* is a perpetual theatrical favorite because it has multiple layers of expertly rendered conflict.

The core story is that the prince, a college student, returns to Denmark and discovers that his uncle Claudius has murdered Hamlet's father, usurped the crown, and married Queen Gertrude, the prince's mother. The prince plots an elaborate revenge intended to reveal Claudius as an assassin, but is racked with self-doubt as he does so.

Hamlet's internal conflict is why the character is a "bucket-list" item for many actors. They hope to find a new wrinkle in one of Western literature's most enduring tales. It's also part of what keeps audiences coming back to see a production that's been done hundreds of times.

But it's not the only reason.

There are many other conflicts in the story, both social and personal. Gertrude has to deal with her complicity in the crime; Claudius wrestles with his guilt; and Hamlet struggles with his would-be girlfriend, Ophelia, plus a terrible showdown with his friend Laertes.

Ophelia departs midway through the story, as does her father, Polonius, presaging more deaths to come. Most of the story's conflicts are resolved by a bloodbath in the court of Castle Elsinore, a culmination that's theatrically satisfying if overwhelmingly depressing.

Nearly as popular as *Hamlet*, *Macbeth* is also full of conflict. The story's eponymous lead character is a war hero who believes a prophecy that he is destined to become king of Scotland. Lady Macbeth believes the prophecy, too—actually more than her husband does—and encourages him to go on a killing spree to make it come true. It's a spree that consumes friends and rivals alike.

The murders roll out one after another, each more horrendous than the last, and as they do, Lady Macbeth descends into madness, overwhelmed with guilt for what she has unleashed. She's a despicable manipulator, but one with great depth, and thus one of Shakespeare's most desirable female roles.

All great stories have conflict: external and internal. External conflict drives dramas and comedies alike. Internal conflict draws readers into the heads and hearts of your story's characters.

The greatest stories combine external and internal conflict so that there is always some degree of tension—during a lull in the battle, a soldier with strong religious convictions questions the morality of what he's doing. Still, when the fighting resumes, he chokes back his doubts and does his duty. Or he puts down his weapon and tells his commanding officer that he can't continue slaughtering other human beings, with potentially dire personal consequences. Or he keeps his convictions to himself and pretends to keep fighting, intentionally missing his targets. Or at a key moment in the battle, he discovers that by making one sure shot, he may be able to spare the lives of hundreds of soldiers on both sides.

Or as happens in Erich Maria Remarque's classic *All Quiet on the Western Front*, he endures the horrors of the entire war only to be killed pointlessly after it is officially ended but before word reaches those on the front lines.

There are many possible outcomes from a single setup.

As a writer of fiction, stage plays, or screenplays, your goal is to take a setup, expand it into a plausible what-if situation, and then insert compelling characters into it. Your fellow fiction writers do this all the time: concoct a plot (plausible or outlandish) and plug in some characters to act it out.

Sounds simple, doesn't it?

Chapter 20

QUIRKY CHARACTERS

Historical upheavals and gut-wrenching personal conflicts aren't the only stories that keep readers turning the pages. Almost as significant are small-scale conflicts—for example, political differences between friends or lifestyle differences between relatives.

Internal inconsistencies—especially self-delusions—are always helpful to make your characters more interesting. The "madness" of King George and the eccentricities of Louis XIV are what make them entertaining. Had they been even-tempered and logical rulers, they would have presided over happier constituents. But they would have been boring to read about, even in biographies, and just about impossible to reconfigure as plausibly amusing characters.

Absent biography fans, many readers aren't interested in "normal" people with "ordinary" lives.

They want to read about wild-and-crazy statistical outliers—explorers, pioneers, geniuses, one-in-a-million talents, lunatics. The business world gushes not about steady-at-the-helm managers but about market disruptors whose inventions and enterprises cause human culture to reorganize itself.

No one wants to read about a career computer programmer who spent years dutifully writing miles of code, but people will flock to so-called "tell-all" books about visionary college dropouts like Steve Jobs and Bill Gates.

Yet interesting characters don't have to be captains of industry or Olympic champions. They may be as simple as neighbors with a running feud, its origins long forgotten, as in the tale of the Hatfields and McCoys, or the Capulet and Montague families in Shakespeare's *Romeo and Juliet*. They don't even remember why they're fighting. Still, the feud gives purpose to their lives, while providing them with opportunities to reconsider their behavior—maybe even to ponder its consequences and to renounce the magnetic attraction of blind stupidity.

Internal quirks make for fascinating characters. Reluctant heroes and charming villains consistently find an eager audience. The James Bond spy franchise always features such villains—twisted geniuses out to conquer or destroy the world, but who cultivate rare orchids or have a special fondness for kittens. Any characteristic that humanizes them makes them more appealing to readers. Heroes that are 100% good are simply dull. So are villains that are 100% evil.

The gray area where they meet is what draws our focus. It's your literary gladiatorial arena.

The quirk of self-delusion is a reliable platform for writing humor and comedy. Consider this fictitious opening:

> *After he retired from the aerospace industry, Uncle*
> *Harry and Aunt Joanie lived in self-imposed squalor.*
> *From the street, their house appeared to be a normal*

middle-class residence, but inside it was a disaster zone of deferred maintenance and botched repairs.

Joanie nagged him constantly about things that needed fixing, but Harry was too proud to call experts. He insisted that he could do it all himself, but despite his engineering credentials, he didn't really know how to handle a screwdriver. He couldn't have replaced a light switch if his life depended on it.

This sort of premise is the basis of *Souvenir*, an outstanding stage play by Stephen Temperley. It follows the career—if she can be said to have had one—of Florence Foster Jenkins, a New York socialite who imagined herself an opera singer and interpreter of classic art songs. Jenkins performed throughout the 1930s and 1940s with her accompanist and loyal friend, Cosmé McMoon, who knew she had a terrible voice but never found the words (or nerve) to tell her.

Jenkins's vainglorious, tone-deaf performances made her a laughingstock of New York society, but she was so deluded that she took audience laughter for approval. As is made clear in the play's touching dénouement, Jenkins was probably incapable of hearing her own voice. She heard it as she imagined it sounding.

Souvenir is also a cautionary tale about how willing people are to indulge the wealthy's vagaries. An old British adage puts it this way: "Madness in a workman is eccentricity in a lord."

Wealthy and powerful characters have much more leeway and enjoy greater forgiveness than do secondary and minor characters, which partly explains their enduring popularity in literature.

From battles among the gods to lifestyles of the rich and famous, it has always been thus.

Chapter 21

NEWS STORIES & OP-EDS

News stories are a special form of writing conveying essential information as succinctly as possible.

The so-called "inverted pyramid" is the traditional, still-applicable structure espoused by generations of journalism instructors. What the phrase means is that informative news stories are written so that the most important aspects are in the lead paragraphs: the "what, where, when, who, why, and how" about what happened.

Sometimes called "front-loading the story," this technique means readers don't need to dig very far to get the essentials:

> *A massive volcano erupted in Indonesia this morning, showering a vast region with lava, ash, and smoke. Dozens of people were killed and thousands displaced by the event, according to reports from Jakarta.*

The ultimate version of such short-form info is the headline: "Massive Volcano Erupts."

(Author's Note: This style of writing was also quite valuable in the early days of radio when announcers would literally "rip-and-read" breaking stories from wire and print news services on the air.)

News reports should be factual and, if possible, based on information from multiple verifiable sources. They should not be peppered with a reporter's subjective opinions or interpretations, unless you're an eyewitness or are interviewing witnesses or experts—in which case, make sure that their comments are correctly attributed. <u>And make sure you have permission to quote them.</u>

Many great writers have worked as news reporters, including Ernest Hemingway and Gabriel García Márquez. Never think that writing news is a low-status gig. It's a respectable occupation that will teach you how to be concise, effective, and efficient. Logging time as a news reporter is excellent training for aspiring writers.

Also, do not be deluded that TV networks, minor-league websites, blogs, or vlogs with explicit political biases are trustworthy sources of information. Many such outlets are simply propaganda organs masquerading as news. While they may occasionally include real coverage to justify their pretense of presenting news, their ultimate purpose is to deceive, manipulate, and inflame an already misinformed audience.

Reliable factual news pieces are as neutral and unbiased as possible and draw on disparate sources. It's a great tradition. Your job as a news reporter is to be neutral and impartial, too, even if the subject of your reporting repels you.

In this regard, opinion pieces and editorials are the opposite of news. Op-ed (opinion and editorial) writers aren't pretending to be objective; they are making statements and observations from obviously biased viewpoints. This is also a respected journalistic tradition—or a despised one, depending on your position. Many writers excel at both reporting news and composing persuasive editorials.

You don't have to be locked into one format or one style. Expanding your literary skills is an exercise in personal and professional freedom.

Chapter 22

AI, PROMISE, AND THREAT

O ver the past few years, concern has mounted over the increasing presence of artificial intelligence (AI). Some pundits are predicting significant job losses as many positions are automated.

As to whether AI will be a boost or a detriment to your career as a writer, the answer depends on your niche in the writing game. If you are generating legal contracts, product warranties, catalog copy, and generic announcements, AI will undoubtedly make your work less tedious. But frankly, it will also eliminate many such positions as AI "authoring" becomes more skilled and its content becomes harder to differentiate from that of humans.

That said, as with spelling and grammar-checking programs (early forms of AI), a sharp-eyed editor will still be at work. A misplaced comma can invalidate a legal contract.

Plus, in some cases, AI-generated language can be unintentionally comical. Many YouTube "documentaries" feature AI-generated narration, with individual words recorded from a live human actor, then strung together by a computer triggered by a written script.

What we hear may sound reasonably cogent, but without natural cadence. The AI interpreter is sometimes stymied by acronyms or unfamiliar text. A short narration may approximate naturalism until it stumbles over "WWII" (World War Two), pronouncing it as *Wuh Wuh Eye-Eye.*

AI will definitely aid in creating everything from the listed ingredients on soup cans to legal boilerplate and prescription medicine brochures and disclaimers. AI will generate many things that people avoid reading.

That said, AI will make certain kinds of projects easier for corporate workers, who will still be plagued by autocorrect errors—a classic trade-off.

Predictably, AI is making incursions into every variety of entertainment, particularly the music industry. Here's Nashville-based music producer Rick Clark discussing the phenomenon with me for the March 2025 issue of *Hi-Fi News*:

> *Typical consumers aren't invested as part of the professional creative class and receive only the end results of years of creative work and practice. As long as what they're hearing or seeing scratches their itch, most people are fine, provided it's free or doesn't cost much.*
>
> *The popular appetite for low-cost entertainment threatens musicians and artists at the bottom of the economy. There will always be creatives, because the need to express will always be there, but AI-generated music, art, video, etc., will become the norm, probably within a decade, conforming to consumers' desired*

effects. Younger generations will have no problem with this because, for them, it will be normal. Eventually, Spotify might decide to farm the elements from millions of pieces of human creativity in order to generate AI music on command.

In time, artists will either have to strike deals with AI operators or find their own human-curated platform— maybe boutique operations for those who value imperfections in real human expression. Music won't die, but it will dramatically change. So will the industries around it.

The arts are canaries in the coal mine. There will be inevitable discord and chaos, but consumers will keep the lights on as they choose between the artificial and the authentic. We overcome fear with adaptability.

Adapt we must. AI is the latest tool to enter the writer's workshop, perhaps the most potent one ever introduced.

Like word processing, it promises to take our profession to a new level, but its all-encompassing nature should be respected. It may prove indispensable as a shortcut to story ideas, plot structures, and, importantly, consistent documentation of essential information, but it will never have wit, insight, or soul. AI may attempt mimicry, but those are human attributes only.

Will AI improve your skills as a journalist, novelist, screenwriter, poet, or songwriter? The jury's still out on that question. Even so, don't be tempted to pass off something generated by an AI tool as your original work. It's not, and you should be professional enough to know better.

The fact remains that the best training for writers in any field is to read extensively, write as much as possible, and learn the essence of editing so that finished pieces deliver maximum impact.

That is the proven, nontechnical path to better writing.

Chapter 23

THE RIGHT WORD IN THE RIGHT SPOT

H ere's a snippet of a news report about the theory that COVID-19 originated in a Chinese laboratory:

The publication of the paper by lead author Li-Meng Yan—an ex-patriot from China seeking asylum in the US—was quickly linked to former White House adviser Steve Bannon, long a strident critic of China's government.

Do you see what's wrong? None of the four writers sharing the byline on this piece, nor the website's editor—if there were one— saw it, either: the description of Li-Meng Yan as "an ex-patriot from China seeking asylum in the US."

While Li-Meng may be an "ex-patriot"—evidenced by the fact that she's seeking asylum away from China—what the authors of this piece meant to say was that she is an *expatriate*, a person living outside her home country. "Expat" is slang for expatriate, as in "Ernest Hemingway lived among American expats in Paris." A related word is *repatriation*, meaning to return displaced people to their native countries, as in "After the war, the French repatriated mercenary troops to West Africa."

The news mistake was probably not noticed by many readers. It's dismaying how few people pay attention to grammar, syntax, spelling, or subject-verb agreement, but that doesn't give you *carte blanche* to be lax about any of it.

One mark of a professional writer is putting the right word in the right spot—and seeing where a better one fits. In the case of *ex-patriot vs. expatriate*, no spelling-and-grammar-checking program in existence would flag either, because both are correct, but one is clearly the better choice.

An astute editor would quickly fix this, elevating the piece from a bit of throwaway journalism into a polished gem. But skilled writers could too—if they were patient and methodical.

Make it part of your work routine to review everything you write so that you're sure about each word. Real writers know how to edit, too.

Chapter 24

TIME'S ON YOUR SIDE

"Time is on my side, yes it is
Time is on my side, yes it is."

—"Time is on My Side," The Rolling Stones, 1965

What are you working on? A news report? A press release? Corporate in-house communications? A short story? A novel?

Each genre of writing has a timeframe or temporal setting—for news, product reviews, press releases, and nearly all corporate writing, the timeframe is the present.

Anything else—celebrity profiles, short stories, screenplays and stage plays, novels—can have any sort of timeframe you wish. A story about a Revolutionary War soldier can be told in the present tense, as if it's a thriller happening now, or as a musty, mostly forgotten detail from the distant past.

As a writer, you have the almost godlike power to reinterpret the past or invent the future. How you choose to do it will determine what sort of audience your work attracts, and maybe how much success you'll have as a careerist in this business.

Shakespeare chose to make the assassination of Roman emperor Julius Caesar a very in-the-moment experience for theatergoers of his time, even though the original events were 1600 years earlier.

Most works of historical fiction do something similar, whereas histories are often tracts of dry facts laid end to end in chronological order so that readers may glean some sense of how long the discussed events lasted, how one led to the next, and how they jointly determined the future.

What sort of period are you trying to cover? A few hours? Days? Years? Or will you shift from one to another as the narrative demands?

Shakespeare's *A Midsummer Night's Dream* takes place in one night; *Hamlet* encompasses a few weeks. They both work beautifully. The implied length of your story's action isn't nearly as important as keeping your readers engaged. "What happens next?" is the driving force of all entertainment—and let's face it, reading is entertainment. If you get your readers to stay with you page after page, you've overcome one of the most significant barriers most writers ever face.

As Syd Field discovered, working as a reader of movie scripts, "Hook 'em up front" is the bylaw of all good writing.

You'll find that the story concept often determines the timespan and the opening and ending points. You'll also find that playing with the chronological order of events can make your writing more engaging.

News stories can be dry as dust or as juicy as a burst watermelon depending on the time perspective—a riot at City Hall could be buried deep in a chronological report of a meeting of the City

Council or could break out as a blockbuster headline: "Police Halt Riot at City Hall."

Select the most essential elements that you're working with and how you want to frame them:

> *Item 14 on the council's agenda had an unexpected result. Townspeople became enraged when the council voted 4-3 to halt repairs to the city's faltering waste treatment plant. . . .*

or

> *At last night's meeting, a negative vote on improving the city's ailing waste treatment plant sparked a spontaneous protest by residents sick of the smell.*

or

> *Police intervened when frustration reached the boiling point for citizens at last night's City Council meeting. . . .*

There's a substantial, dramatic difference in each recitation of the same information.

Timeframe for writers is a highly elastic concept. You may cover the entirety of the Hundred Years' War in one sentence, or you may take a clue from Argentine writer Ernesto Sabato, who filled the first forty-some pages of his novel *The Angel of Darkness* with descriptions of what his main character encounters and feels as he walks down a city street—in this case, events that take almost as long to read about as to experience in real life.

Time may be your biggest aggravation—as in having to meet a deadline—but as a pliable element, it's among the most valuable instruments in the writer's gig bag.

Chapter 25

YOU DON'T HAVE TO BE A VIRTUOSO

Received wisdom holds that successful writers are gifted geniuses, rare specimens endowed with exceptional talent.

An hour spent in any library or bookstore will prove how wrong this is. You don't have to be a virtuoso to enjoy a rewarding career as a writer. You don't even have to be a superb writer to succeed.

You simply have to be competent and consistent.

Virtuosity, in fact, may limit your appeal, especially among American readers steeped in simple narrative-and-dialog style. True literary geniuses such as Gabriel Garcia Marquez (*One Hundred Years of Solitude, Love in the Time of Cholera*) and Cormac McCarthy (*Child of God, The Orchard Keeper, All the Pretty Horses*) have legions of loyal fans, aesthetes who love their tumbling play of images and their unexpected descriptions and associations, but their astounding literary abilities present difficulties for ordinary readers.

Their books will always have an eager audience, but in terms of sales, they can't compare to the works of pop writers such as Sidney

Sheldon, author of more than a dozen novels. Here's a sample plucked more-or-less at random from the middle of his *The Best Laid Plans*, published in 1997:

> *Friday night, Dana was seated next to Jeff Connors in the press box at Camden Yards, watching the baseball game. And for the first time since she had returned, she was able to think about something other than the war. As Dana watched the players on the field, she listened to the announcer reporting the game.*

Simple style, simple vocabulary. Nothing elaborate that would force readers to pick up the dictionary. Sheldon would never use "avaricious" instead of "greedy," nor "quotidian" instead of "daily." His purpose is to present a tale about ordinary people in a comfortably conversational style.

Most best-selling novels and almost all general-interest non-fiction works are presented in a conversational tone: blockbuster best-sellers such as Erich Segal's *Love Story* or Robert James Waller's *The Bridges of Madison County* are written in this tone, with storyline and character development sufficient to sustain readers' interest.

Conversational tone also sustains *What Doesn't Kill You*, a novel about a forty-something single mom reinventing herself in the business world, jointly authored by Virginia DeBerry and Donna Grant:

> *So I threw myself into mounting my career campaign— sounded a lot like war. I realized later it was. I worked to assess my on-the-job strengths, analyze my skills, define my objectives—it felt a lot like I was back in the guidance counselor's office, and I wasn't sure I had any more idea what I wanted to be when I grew up than I did then.*

The book adheres to this style throughout its nearly 300 pages.

Some very successful writers simplify almost to the point of absurdity. James Ellroy is a master of the staccato tough-guy voice of mid-century crime fiction. A tidbit from his enduringly popular *American Tabloid*:

> *The hut was matchbook-size. He had to cram the table and two chairs in... Kemper handled Gordean with kid gloves. The interrogation dragged—his subject had the DTs.*

Compare this to the lyrical style of Michael Ondaatje's *The English Patient*:

> *He walks with her through the indigo markets that lie between South Cairo and her home. The beautiful songs of faith enter the air like arrows, one minaret answering another, as if passing on a rumour of the two of them as they walk through the cold morning air, the smell of charcoal and hemp already making the air profound. Sinners in a holy city.*

This is no simple sketch of two people walking along. In this elegant passage, Ondaatje evokes sight, sound, scent, ambiguity, and potentiality with exquisite skill: indigo markets, songs like arrows, profound air—allusions that work beautifully for readers attuned to nuance.

New York Times art critic Michael Kimmelman strikes a lovely balance between lyricism and straightforward journalism in his book *The Accidental Masterpiece: On the Art of Life and Vice Versa*. Here's his background description of the contentious fate of Philadelphia's Barnes Collection, established by eccentric doctor

Albert C. Barnes and bequeathed to a school in Chester County, Pennsylvania:

> (He) amassed great Cézanne's, Matisse's, and African art, along with metal knickknacks and folk doodads like door locks and a tiny sculpture in the shape of a cricket. Famously, he displayed these all together in a mansion outside Philadelphia, in odd, mixed-up arrangements seemingly arbitrary to the uninitiated... Nobody looked at art the way Barnes did. Self-taught in this regard, from a working-class background, having earned his way through medical school playing professional baseball, he developed an enormous chip on his shoulder toward what he considered the art establishment, and he feuded publicly with anyone he thought hoity-toity.

That's Kimmelman simply providing background, and it's a delight to read. He might have simplified it for ordinary readers or gussied it up for art-world academics, but instead, he took the middle path and crafted his work to reach the largest audience.

Chapter 26

YOUR WORK HABITS

H ow do you approach a writing project? Do you do a lot of research and take many notes? Do you work up an outline and several backstories? Or do you simply plow forth with a head full of ideas and let what you're composing guide you?

There are as many ways to work as there are people to do it. Some writers are extremely disciplined: the novelist John Updike reputedly got up each morning and wrote for four hours before doing anything else. Stephen King reportedly has a similar habit.

Others are more haphazard. Some carry little reporter's notebooks and make notes throughout the day or recite messages to themselves into their phones.

It's safe to say that most professional writers are adept with computers and are comfortable with word-processing programs such as Microsoft Word. Most of us have—or should have, as an occupational requirement—the ability to type quickly and accurately. Some are hunt-and-peck typists, as often depicted in films by actors pretending to be writers. (Actually, the actors are probably hunt-and-peck typists, too.)

Herb Caen, the legendary columnist for the *San Francisco Chronicle*, was a proud two-finger hunt-and-peck writer. Some esteemed old-school writers did their work totally in longhand. Novelist Kurt Vonnegut (*Cat's Cradle*) was one. Asked by an interviewer whether he used a computer, he reportedly said no—he wrote everything longhand on legal pads and, when he had enough pages, sent them to an assistant to be transcribed.

If you don't know how to type, there are many typing tutorials available. Don't hesitate to learn—it's a valuable (and timesaving) skill. There are also many voice recognition programs that turn your speech into text, but you'll still need to format and edit the results to appear and read the way you want. Moreover, if you're an expert typist, you may not react well to trying to adapt to voice recognition. In my experience, the internal voice is different from the spoken voice.

Your hours are your own. Updike may have been an early-morning whirlwind, but for each one like him, many others do their best work at night. Some have found that late-night fatigue is a strong motivator for creative projects.

My advice? Find what works for you and stick with it. Here's further advice from Charles McNair, an international business communication consultant, award-winning journalist, cultural critic, columnist, and novelist. His most recent novel, *The Epicureans*, was serialized on the website *The Bitter Southerner*. McNair lives and works in Bogotá, Colombia.

> *Creating a habit of writing makes a difference. A million distractions that all seem important will duck-bite a whole day away, then another, and another, without the resolve to write.*

Resolve, it turns out, can be habituated. Tricks to create a habit? As with flossing or exercising, the mind will miss rituals when they're skipped. So, create rituals for writing: A cup of coffee with the first words of the day. A song to serve as the soundtrack for a particular piece. (A friend who wrote a book set in Germany fired up Mozart as she sat down to work each day.) Light a candle to invoke the muse.

The easiest way is simply to commit to sitting for five minutes each day – just five. If you're stubborn, you'll do five, then get up and go away. The next day, you'll hardheadedly sit for five more. Then you'll be ashamed that yesterday's five and this day's five add up to zero words, and you'll put down the truest sentence you know, then go away.

Next day, five more...a habit is forming now...and you have a place to start, an actual sentence to build on. And so, it goes.

Next? What's a word count per day you can successfully meet? That's your next goal. Your realistic goal. You are not Jack London, and you're most likely not going to write 6,000 words a day. If that's your goal, again, most likely, you're setting yourself up to fail, not to succeed. I think anybody can write a page a day. That's 365 pages, one book, every year.

Bottom line? Incrementalism is in the bones of writers. So...a page a day? Five hundred words a day? One thousand words a day (about four pages), that's been my goal for the past month. Again, the point is to make goals you can meet. Otherwise, the failed word counts can defeat writerly ambition.

Finally, steal insanely and joyfully, but do yourself a favor: do so from the best. Once you determine you'll write, shamelessly ape the style, plot, vocabulary, and all of the writer you most want to be when you finally make it as a writer. Take a book by James Joyce or James Patterson and put it by the computer and type, word-for-word, on your own screen, the story he's written. You'll be amazed at how clearly you can see how a character enters, how a character is described, and how a plot moment happens.

You won't ever be the writer you mimic...but you'll turn these lessons into the writer that's your own good self.

Chapter 27

"WRITING FOR THE BYLINE" AND OTHER SCAMS

An old joke defines the difference between amateur and professional writers. The amateur asks, "When do I get published?" The professional asks, "When do I get paid?"

Sooner or later, every beginning writer will fall for a variation on one of the oldest scams in the publishing industry: *writing for the byline*. This means not getting paid in actual currency, but somehow enjoying the reward of seeing one's name attached as the author of a published piece. Such acknowledgment is, of course, validation—but it does not pay the bills.

Personal anecdote time: My several part-time gigs include working as an arts writer and theatre critic for Marin County's daily newspaper. An annual early-summer event in Marin County is the Mountain Play, typically a classic blockbuster musical at the old amphitheater on Mount Tamalpais. In years past, sponsors of the show would host a meet-and-greet luncheon a couple of weeks before the show's opener, with plenty of good food and drinks, a pep talk by some show officials, and a few songs by some of the cast—a delightful way to spend an afternoon.

At one such event, I was seated near a woman who published a neighborhood newspaper for the wealthiest parts of San Francisco. I was vaguely familiar with her publication. Full of ads for hair and nail salons, trendy boutiques, healers and therapists of every imaginable variety, interior designers, and upscale remodeling contractors, her newspaper was most definitely a for-profit enterprise. Toward the end of lunch, she not-so-deftly asked if I might be interested in contributing to her publication.

I replied, "Maybe. First, we have to discuss compensation."

She went red in the face and blurted out this indignation: "I don't pay my contributors! They work for the byline."

My retort: "How nice. You're getting what you're paying for. And they are getting what they deserve."

I would not have been so curt if she had asked me to support philanthropic efforts for disabled orphans. We should all be willing to aid the needy. For-profit enterprises don't qualify for charity.

If they're making money from your work, <u>you deserve a cut.</u>

Working for the byline has been a lure for writers since before the internet era, but it has reached epidemic proportions today. The current version of this scam is *building your brand*—the pitch that getting your name out there will somehow magically translate into more work, eventually leading to actual pay.

While this may prove true in a small minority of cases, it's a cynical ploy to get writers, photographers, graphic artists, and other creatives to supply "content" for websites whose real purpose is to carry as much advertising as possible. Publishers may encourage you to keep feeding the machine, cheering you on about how many drive-by views you're getting, or how many mouse clicks, or how many repostings. Bushwa.

In the first dot-com era, one prominent news site (its name is irrelevant) rose from nothing to a multimillion-dollar enterprise partly by promising unpaid contributors that they would share revenue once the site reached profitability. Contributors got nothing during the site's growth cycle but kept working like donkeys pursuing elusively tantalizing carrots. Predictably, they also got nothing when the site was sold for a seven-figure profit.

Don't take the bait. Make sure you have a compensation agreement up front.

Chapter 28

PAY SCALE

How much can you expect to earn as a professional writer? That all depends on where you land on the enormous—and enormously steep—pyramid that is the writing profession. It's "enormously steep" because the base of this pyramid consists of unpaid or underpaid writers toiling away at websites and small-circulation publications. In contrast, the tip of the pyramid is occupied by the lucky few with blockbuster novels or screenplays.

Most websites and blogs are labors of love sustained by enthusiasts. Small-circulation periodicals, such as many local newspapers and special-interest journals, do pay their contributors, but their fee structures are often decades out of date.

You may hone your skills working for such enterprises, but you'll need a day job to support yourself while doing so. Most writing is a fee-for-service business, like plumbing. You do the job and collect the check. Throughout the 20th century, most respectable publications had salaried writers on staff, a species almost extinct today. With few exceptions, nearly everyone now does piecework. Piecework was also common during the glory days of American journalism. Newspaper columnists may not have made much per piece, but if they were syndicated in a couple of hundred newspapers, they enjoyed tremendous paydays.

Websites may pay anywhere from nothing to a couple of hundred dollars for a published piece—especially if they have advertising or subscriber support. Local newspapers are similar—perhaps a flat fee of $75 to $100 for each piece, or they may have a "per word" or "word rate" of so many cents per word, based on the word count of the edited final.

Monthly journals offer better compensation, such as a flat fee of $500 for a one-page editorial or $1,200 for a multipage in-depth story, plus an additional stipend for the rights to reproduce your work online. Beware the phrase "for use in perpetuity" in any contract, as it may preclude you from reusing the same material.

Publications may accept and run your work without asking for a contract—if so, you retain the intellectual property rights. Contracts signed with publications that subsequently go out of business are probably invalid. Should this issue ever arise for you, seek advice from a publishing industry attorney.

At the top of the economic pyramid are authors of blockbuster novels, screenplays, and stage plays. You are not likely to be the next Danielle Steel or Lin-Manuel Miranda and shouldn't pin your hopes on an unattainable dream. As a broad generalization, most novels don't sell in large numbers, and few stage plays make significant money, apart from long-running multinational hits like *Hamilton*.

Screenplays are an interesting exception in that you can make quite a decent living writing them, even if your name never appears onscreen. Film production companies stockpile promising scripts in anticipation of trends—if "robotic-dinosaurs-rampaging-on-the-moon" looks like the next big thing, they can go to their archives, pull out some promising scripts with that theme, and toss them around for possible production.

The film and television industry supports an underground economy of "script doctors," specialists in tweaking scripts with promising premises but perhaps lacking character development or believable dialogue. The fact that so many bad films and TV shows see the light of day is proof that this is a ripe market for talented writers. Simply be aware that a script is a blueprint for a production rather than a work of literary art, and once you've sold it, it's no longer yours.

There are some lucrative but obscure niches in the writing game, mostly unknown to the general public. Ghostwriting is a good one.

Today, many celebrities and business executives want a book to their credit. Even though they may be capable of writing such books, they usually don't actually write them. They don't have the time. Their books are written by trusted contractors who interview their subjects, do the needed research, and submit their work for the client's approval. Professional editors tweak the final.

Many ghostwritten books sell well, and their invisible authors enjoy income and the likelihood of further work from having done them. You aren't likely to land a ghostwriting gig simply by walking in the door and asking for it. A more substantial possibility is a recommendation from a colleague or a colleague's friend.

Career speechwriter Ken Askew, with dozens of high-level clients in his Rolodex, has this to say about this niche of the writing game:

> *Ghostwriting isn't limited to vanity books; indeed, that's a small percentage of the craft. I've ghosted countless WSJ, NYT, WaPo, etc. op-eds for various executives and politicians, magazine articles in various think-tank*

publications, and several long-running editorial gigs (for instance, weekly syndicated columns for medical and education thought-leaders that went on for years)–all without editorial credit, which was just dandy with me.

The several books I've ghostwritten–the 100-year anniversary history of a Fortune 50 company, after close to a year of travel and hundreds of interviews; an inside view of migrating traditional financial services into the digital age, after spending 24/7 with a CEO and his closest advisor; a best-selling how-we-did-it yarn (and great story) by an OG 'rock star' CEO; a passionate plea by a thought leader for reviving STEM education on the scale prompted by the Russian Sputnik "threat" in the 1960s–all these projects were individually distinctive and not crammed into one general niche, much less what you'd call vanity fluff.

Many ghostwriting careers germinate in government, often at various White House Cabinet support roles– hard-core researchers churning out white papers in obscurity for Departments of State, Health & Human Services, Energy, Transportation, Education, and so on, funneled to speechwriters in what's essentially a farm system for future ghostwriters.

All of this is to say that ghostwriting is actually one of the most reasonable ways to make a good living doing quality work with repeat clientele, largely based on earned relationships through specialized knowledge, the ability to ask smart questions, and the ability to listen analytically. It involves becoming conversant about issues at a high level in a given field and developing a reputation for informed judgment that can be trusted by subject-matter experts. It requires being able to hold your own in substantive conversation with them so they're comfortable allowing you some agency in representing their voice.

This may not sound sexy or glamorous, but if you are talking about actually getting paid and reliably covering the rent, it's gold.

> (Author's Note: Gold for talented individuals. A couple of seasons ago, the popular TV show Shark Tank featured an entrepreneur from a company called "Business Ghost," a service for people seeking ghostwriters. His pitch to potential investors was that he had a team of writers to tackle any project. He promised a quick turnaround and a polished product, but was unable to generate interest among the show's billionaires.

Two women with a similar concept, "My Wonderful Life," also got rebuffed by the Sharks. Their concept was a sort of instant memorial service, in which the bereaved or the about-to-be-deceased would send biographical details, names of favorite films and music, photos, video clips, etc., and these two women would piece together a compelling story. It sounded like a good plan. All the Sharks admitted that yes, everyone will die eventually, but because they couldn't imagine a way to scale up the service, they bowed out of investing.)

Speechwriting is a highly specialized and well-compensated niche that demands a keen ear for the intended speaker's voice, mannerisms, and intellectual level, and an understanding of the audience for which the speech is intended. A group of MIT scientists is vastly different from a group of union steelworkers. The speechwriter's goal is to fade into the background while making the client look as authentic as possible.

Ghostwriting and speechwriting are two specialties that writers fall into more or less by accident. There's no school to teach you how to do this. Referrals for such work are likely to come your way through the most unexpected doors.

The next chapter includes an amusing tale by and about Askew, who became a top-tier talent exactly that way.

Chapter 29

SPEECHES

L ike dialogue in plays and films, speeches are intended to be heard, not read. A well-crafted speech considers the speaker's voice and accent, the subjects to be addressed, the estimated length of the speech, and the audience that will hear it.

With more than forty years' experience in the political and corporate trenches, career speechwriter Ken Askew is an expert at all this. Before writing the first draft, he interviews new clients to get a handle on their personalities and styles.

He knows better than to try to make a Texas oilman sound like a Stanford professor. He also knows how much detail and humor to throw into each piece, and does not suffer from pangs of prima donna resentment if a client goes off-script and ignores most of his carefully crafted work. That's all part of the game.

The following story about the travails of a speechwriter with a new giant-sized client was excerpted from a 2003 edition of *Vital Speeches of the Day*. It's a cautionary tale for newbies, and one hilarious read from start to finish, especially the introduction included here:

Former White House speechwriter Ken Askew has served as a senior staff speechwriter for U.S. President George H. W. Bush, U.S. Senator Sam Nunn (D-GA), Chrysler executives Lee Iacocca, Jerry Greenwald, and Bob Lutz, and BellSouth Chairman John Clendenin. In subsequent consultancy, he has written for more than thirty-five Fortune 200 chairmen and CEOs worldwide. Askew operates a private communication consultancy and is associated with The White House Writers Group in Washington, D.C.

How do you write for President George H. W. Bush, Lee Iacocca, Roberto Goizueta, and Sam Nunn?

Very carefully.

"Confessions of a Wounded Speechwriter"
By Ken Askew

Our plan is simple. As speechwriters, we will engage the imaginations of our clients, provoke from them substance, add texture, and convey to the world an enriched wisdom. Will our plan run into trouble?

BIG TROUBLE.

My big trouble with speeches began in 1985, when I was hired as Senator Sam Nunn's scribe. First assignment: Address the Trilateral Commission about mutual assured destruction. Yow!

There was little I knew less about, so I visited the venue for inspiration: a stately D.C. mansion converted to a museum. The Senator was to speak in a splendid dining hall sagging with art treasures: Matisse, Gauguin, Picasso, de Kooning, Cézanne, and Rubens.

To capture the sinister logic of nuclear strategy, I built the speech around a line from poet Kenneth Rexroth, "Art is the reasoned derangement of the senses," and adorned it with properly spirited quotes from artists represented in the room—such as Cézanne's "I close my eyes that I might see."

Each quote was associated with a painting, all except Rubens' "The Repentant Peter", showing the contrite disciple grieving at Christ's crucifixion—abstractions with little to suggest their titles. So, I drew a podium guide: The Picasso is at your three o'clock, Senator; the de Kooning to your nine. All nested in nine pages of textured prose that (in retrospect) only Gauloises-sucking Soho denizens in black mock-turtlenecks and berets might countenance.

The big event arrived. It was a dark and stormy night. Pouring rain; the Senate locked in a vote; an agitated Sam Nunn bursting from the Capitol portico an hour late. We piled into the car; from the front seat, I introduced myself as the new speechwriter and handed the Senator his draft. Flip. Flip. Flip. Flip...flip. Flip... flip...flip. "Did you write this?" he asked.

Tension was palpable. The Senator urged speed and asked for proper pronunciation of Matisse. Charlie Harmon, senior aide at the wheel, reluctantly ran red lights, which is legal for senators in an official hurry in D.C. Stupidly searching for soothing music, I turned on the radio and a "Hooked on Classics" disco version of "Barber of Seville" blared forth like a cartoon soundtrack.

When we arrived, dessert was ancient history, and the Senator bounded to the podium. I took my seat between a Rockefeller and a former national security advisor, who by now were restlessly inspecting their forks and spoons.

And the bolt then hit me. The podium had been moved! My Art Map for the Senator was wrong! Coordinates could not be trusted! Ye gods, Senator, Matisse occupies Picasso territory!

I grabbed linen and ruined it with large letters: Senator! The Art Has Moved! and desperately waved for his attention, attracting only disdain from the Rockefeller flank. The Senator, for his part, disregarded my wretched demi-semaphore, glanced about the room, waved at several pals who help lead the free world, nailed a joke about Noah vis-à-vis the torrent outside, and launched into thirty unrehearsed minutes of for the life of me I know not what. Heads bobbed in sober excitement, muted voices murmured; no mutual destruction was as assured as mine because I did not recognize the language my new client was using as English. It was instead a lofty techno-patois of code-speak grokked apparently only by, say, the Beast-marked Trilateral Commission and cryptic folk who hang out at the Pentagon.

Suddenly, the Senator stopped. Dramatic pause. For the first time, he consulted his prepared remarks, and gesturing toward the lone conceptually recognizable work hanging in the room–the Rubens–said with measured deliberation, "Looking at that 'Repentant Peter', I'm reminded of the quote, art is the reasoned derangement of the senses."

It's a tough quote to say and hear, but he delivered it perfectly, enunciating the colliding "Ds." He looked around the room. "And you know, our topic tonight is kind of like that." He had the instinct to let it bloom.

The thought moved through the room like big weather. His audience nodded and susurrated agreement. Our good Senator tied up his remarks with a ribbon and got a standing ovation.

And the speechwriter? Saved by a pro.

On the ride home, the Senator was in a fine mood. He said to me, "Good quote," and meant it.

We worked together well for a year or so. Then came "The College Graduation Speech." To Georgia Tech, no less, and the Senator is a Bee.

> (Author's Note: Georgia Tech athletic teams are "The Yellow Jackets." GT students and grads are therefore "Bees". But I digress.)

I took the opportunity to write the speech I wished to hear, which was a high-profile suggestion to young graduates that this might be a swell time to take off a couple of years and skylark for pocket change: Wait tables in Istanbul. Ride a motorcycle across Africa. Play blues piano in a Honolulu honky-tonk. Sail an unstable antique yawl around the world. Not understanding the *speech was a personal vindication for my own post-collegiate misbehavior, Nunn called me into his office after reading the first draft.*

The Senator was not whistling "The Happy Wanderer."

"Ken," he said, "if I delivered this speech, all the parents in the stands who have paid good money to send their kids to Tech would rise up and lynch me."

I rewrote, suggesting an immediate search for responsible jobs. And soon thereafter left political speechwriting for a great long while, taking with me the humbling lessons: Write their heart, not yours; and style is fine, but you gotta have substance.

Chapter 30

THE PUBLISHING ECOSYSTEM

Have you ever wondered about all the names that appear on a publication's masthead? What do their titles mean, and what do they do?

In American magazines, the masthead is usually a few pages beyond the front cover, often near the table of contents. In a typical newspaper, the masthead may be somewhere in the first few pages, or it may be on or near the editorial section. It's a list of all the most important people involved in producing each issue—perhaps not all, but most.

Publications have two distinct branches: publishing and editorial. Publishing is the business end: physical and digital production, payroll, printing, advertising, subscriptions, distribution, and legalities. The publisher oversees all of this. The publisher has many assistants to ensure everything runs smoothly, including advertising sales representatives, subscription managers, and a team of digital specialists who continually update the publication's website.

Editorial is the content department, including feature stories, news items, opinion pieces, event calendars, photos, graphs, and artwork—everything that appears in a publication other than advertising. The editor in chief oversees all of this and steers story development to ensure continued reader interest and, thus, a predictable number of readers that ad reps can point to when pitching contracts to potential advertisers.

You may have noticed that the annual subscription rate for many magazines is less than the cost of a single issue at a newsstand. This is an intentional marketing ploy—a publication with a subscription base of 80,000 readers and newsstand sales of 10,000 per month means that if each issue gets shared a little bit, that publication can justifiably claim a monthly readership in excess of 100,000.

Many special-interest publications, such as automotive magazines, have explicit, well-publicized "separation of church and state" policies that aim to reassure readers that advertising contracts don't influence their product reviews. In other words, *Car and Driver* may sell ad space to Toyota, but is under no obligation to run favorable reviews of Toyota products. Reviewers are therefore free to make objective evaluations.

This principle is often violated among small-circulation special-interest titles. It is discouragingly common, which is why endorsements from internet influencers are not entirely trustworthy.

Pay-to-play is a foregone conclusion with many websites, especially those with no visible advertising revenue. Any publication involving reviews of expensive products should have its objectivity questioned, because there is a delicate diplomatic dance involved in arranging loans of review units.

The only publication to have found a way around this potential public relations nightmare is *Consumer Reports*, which does not accept samples to review but instead buys them at retail.

The editor in chief has a primary assistant, the managing editor, who does all of the nuts-and-bolts work of putting each issue together: riding herd on contributors (variously called correspondents, contributing writers, contributing editors, etc.), making sure that they are on schedule with works in progress, and supervising photography, artwork, and layout of each piece. Proofreaders—really, entry-level copyeditors—scour submitted text for spelling, punctuation, and subject/verb agreement. Journeymen copyeditors work on submitted pieces to improve narrative flow and concision and may alter text to conform to "house style," assuming their publication has one.

The next level up from copyediting is ghostwriting (see earlier chapter), fairly common in book publishing but unusual in newspapers and magazines, except for op-ed pieces submitted to business publications and major papers. An op-ed by a CEO in the *Wall Street Journal* was likely written by someone on the CEO's staff or by an outside contractor. Books by celebrity authors often credit the ghostwriter ("with Joan Robertson"), but sometimes don't. Ghostwritten books are usually 98% the work of the ghostwriter, with the celebrity making suggestions and approving the final project.

An editor at large may be a semiretired or legendary journalist who still makes occasional contributions—the publishing world's equivalent of a professor emeritus, one who put in long years, achieved some notoriety, and still maintains an office on campus, but is free of the obligation to teach classes or produce research.

Graphic designers go by many titles (including layout artist) and are adept with programs such as InDesign that let them wrap photos with text to guide readers from the opening headline to the closing statement. Book designers do this on a larger scale, specialty cousins to the layout artists of the periodical world.

Surprising to new writers is the fact that most of the people whose names appear on a masthead don't work in a bustling newsroom, something that's increasingly an artifact of old movies. Most contributors work remotely. Today, only a few people can be found in any publication's home office.

Not significant in the world of periodicals, but hugely important in marketing books, screenplays, and stage plays, are literary agents and agencies, managers, attorneys, and public relations specialists. If you are far enough along with such a project, you have probably met some of these folks.

If not, you will. They're waiting for you. It's simply a matter of time.

Chapter 31

PROFILES AND PREVIEWS

A "profile" is a journalistic sketch of a personality, typically peppered with biographical details and observations made by a writer who's spent time with the subject of the story—a couple of hours, a day, or a week.

Details about the subject don't have to be exhaustive, but they need to be sufficient to convey some sense of who the subject is and what he or she is doing. Don't burden readers with more than they want to know. Include just enough to whet their appetites.

A "preview" is a story about an upcoming event. Often, details about such events are supplied in press releases provided by press agents. Feel free to lift information from press releases and include it in your piece. That's what press releases are for.

Profiles typically run 1,000–2,000 words; previews can be much shorter, 500–1,000 words. The two can sometimes be combined into one piece, as in the following example, a 20-year-old *Pacific Sun* story about actor/magician Ron Severdia.

"Renaissance Man"
By Barry Willis

Ron Severdia is a risk taker.

Imagine being locked in a wooden shipping crate thrown into the near-freezing Danube River in a re-enactment of one of Harry Houdini's most dangerous stunts. Imagine further making a successful escape from the sinking crate, only to have it fill up with water to the point that it was too heavy to pull back onto the bridge from which it fell.

Severdia, who's done the stunt in the chilly San Francisco Bay—without the near-death experience—floated for two hours in the cold current while cameras rolled, waiting to be rescued. The hypothermia he suffered was a small price to pay for the notoriety gained, says the Mill Valley actor.

In the four days before Christmas, Severdia will take risks of a different sort, in a one-man performance of Charles Dickens' "A Christmas Carol" at Ross Valley Players.

Inspired in part by legendary solo shows such as James Whitmore's interpretation of Will Rogers, and Hal Holbrook's embodiment of Mark Twain, Severdia won't become one character, but many: the embittered miser Ebenezer Scrooge, Scrooge's departed business partner Jacob Marley, the hapless accountant Bob Cratchit, Cratchit's crippled son Tiny Tim, and the ghosts of

Christmas past, present, and future—more than forty characters in all.

Severdia will dig deep into his extensive bag of tricks to make the story come to life. Although the show will include a guest appearance by Robert Young, who for years has appeared as Charles Dickens at the "Great Dickens Christmas Fair," Severdia will also serve as narrator, using text adapted from Dickens' novel. Scene and character transitions will be accomplished with simple blocking and lighting shifts, sound effects, changes in voice and intonation, a handful of props, costume elements by Michael Berg—and a healthy dollop of sleight of hand.

He'll come to the challenge well prepared. An accomplished magician by the age of nine, Severdia studied at College of Marin with legendary director Jim Dunn and at the American Conservatory Theater. He's especially proud of a Shakespearean certification ("with distinction") from London's Royal Academy of Dramatic Art.

A Marin County native, the multitalented/multilingual Severdia has tread a circuitous route: childhood in Novato, high school years in Santa Cruz (where he performed street magic), to the American Bartending School, to Louisiana State University, where he got a degree in marketing.

In 1994, he finished his TOEFL (Test of English as a Foreign Language) certification and moved to Vienna, Austria, where he began teaching English at the British Embassy. He reworked a play he had written and performed about Houdini and put it on in Bratislava, Slovakia, and at the International Theater of Vienna.

His escape stunt on the Danube generated plenty of press and television exposure, giving Severdia enough leverage to start the Bratislava English Theatre. He performed in English-language theatrical productions and festivals in Vienna, Paris, Berlin, and London.

In 1997, Severdia started a small ad agency in Bratislava, focused on helping local businesses translate campaigns for European markets. A local restaurateur approached him about opening an American restaurant, which they ran together for a few years. He returned to the Bay Area near the end of the first dot-com era and worked at various ad agencies doing design and art direction, and returned to the Bay Area theatre scene in "Room Service" at RVP in 2004.

Multiple expertise, wide experience, and an unfettered imagination make him one of our most versatile local actors.

Severdia combines an accessible affability with a deft sense of comic timing. Like Dan Aykroyd and John Goodman, he's one of those actors who's funny just standing there. His imposing physical presence, deferential demeanor, and razor-sharp but indirect wit very much suggest an offensive lineman from any Southern college football team—the easygoing workhorse who doesn't take the game too seriously, whose wry one-liners keep his teammates and coaches chuckling through the most grueling practices.

That's the sort of typecasting he hopes to grow out of—what he calls "village idiot roles," Severdia said over a recent lunch at "Rafters" in San Rafael.

The actor himself may dismiss such parts, but from the audience's perspective he's brilliant. Severdia was a standout as the kindhearted Southern simpleton Ellard Simms, opposite Edwin Richards in Ross Valley Players' uproarious production of "The Foreigner", and did a wonderful turn as houseboy Ito in Novato Theater Company's run of "Mame" last year.

He followed that with a strong dramatic role in RVP's "Wait Until Dark", did another comic turn in Marin Shakespeare Company's "Knight of the Burning Pestle", then took on another serious part in Marin Shakes' "King Lear".

Severdia has the distinction of having played the lead in Exit Theater's controversial reverse-cast production of "Othello", as well as having played Iago in the Vienna Shakespeare Festival's English-language production of the same play. Few actors have played both parts.

Severdia's one-man "A Christmas Carol" took root several years ago but didn't begin to sprout until last summer. He had written a script that, while remaining true to Dickens' original, deleted much of its superfluous and tangential material. Paring the story down to its essential elements was the first step toward bringing it to the stage.

The next was shaping it into something that would be dramatically compelling, neither too truncated nor overly long. Severdia began performing snippets of his show-to-be at San Francisco's Marsh Theater, drawing the attention of veteran performer and theater coach Charlie Varon, who among other specialties conducts workshops for standup comedians and solo performers.

Varon was instrumental in transforming "A Christmas Carol" from a work in progress to a real dramatic production, the actor acknowledges. "He's very good at giving perspective," says Severdia.

One Monday night, actor and veteran director (California Shakespeare Festival, San Jose Repertory, Marin Theater Company) Julian Lopez-Morillas saw his performance and was so taken that he volunteered to direct. That freed Severdia from a least one task (he's also functioning as producer, sound designer, and graphic/web designer for the show) so that he could focus on refining his script and rehearsing it.

Morillas has been invaluable in the process, Severdia says. Despite the profit potential and promotional value of recording "A Christmas Carol", Severdia won't attempt to produce videos of his live show—at least not this time. "There's only so much of me to go around," he jokes.

Putting a fresh spin on a perennial favorite is a daunting, ambitious project. Like many of Shakespeare's most popular works, the Dickens classic has been mounted innumerable times for the stage, and remade dozens of times as feature films and made-for-TV specials.

Leaping into a freezing river in a sealed box may have garnered Severdia extended opportunities in Eastern Europe, but a superb solo show could launch his American career in entirely new directions.

If a November preview performance is anything to go by, Ron Severdia's "A Christmas Carol" should be one to remember.

Chapter 32

BASICS OF REVIEWING, PART ONE

D o you have a special interest? A sport, an art, a craft? Do you have an ongoing affair with technological devices such as cameras, bicycles, or cars?

If so, you may be a potential reviewer. You don't need academic credentials to write for most publications, but you do need deep experience in the field you want to cover. A PhD in literature probably won't help much if you are going to review novels, but a lifetime of reading them certainly will.

If you want to write about cars, you don't need a degree in automotive engineering. Still, you do need an enormous volume of knowledge about cars and the automotive business—all the myriad details that enthusiasts absorb from every possible source and eagerly share with like-minded friends.

In reviewing a vehicle, you'll need to convey how it performs compared to competitors, knowledge that can be gained only behind the wheel.

Professional reviewers for publications such as *Road & Track* or *Car and Driver* evaluate vehicles loaned to them by manufacturers. In contrast, amateur reviewers try to gather as much information as possible by posing as customers and test-driving vehicles from dealers' lots.

A substantial niche of the publishing industry known as "enthusiast" titles, automotive magazines are excellent sources for learning how to write concise, comprehensive, and entertaining reviews.

Every month, *Road and Track* and *Car and Driver* run multiple reviews of new cars—each piece describing the vehicle's concept, place in the overall market, fit, finish, features, handling, price, and value. Directed toward a casual readership of people in the market for new vehicles, these reviews are usually breezy but exhaustive—a difficult combination for most writers. They tell potential buyers almost everything they need to know to decide on a new car—often in just one or two superbly crafted pages, with room for a couple of high-resolution photos.

Readers of such product reviews may not be auto-journal subscribers but are simply trying to educate themselves before making a major purchase. Enthusiast publications also run longer, in-depth pieces directed toward their core readership—profiles of industry legends and famous drivers, tours of automotive museums, histories of rare vehicles, and sometimes even humorous pieces about cars that never went into production or whose production was halted after only a few months because of multiple mechanical problems or serious liability issues.

A real treat is the rare piece about a vehicle whose fundamental concept was so flawed that it became legendary for all the wrong reasons.

The Trabant was one such car, produced in East Germany during the Cold War, from 1957 to 1990. Widely regarded as one of the worst cars ever made—a surprisingly large category—it was an object of ridicule in the West but of desire for East German workers, who had to wait ten years or longer to buy one. Dangerous, poorly designed, with little power and few comforts for passengers, the "Trabi" had body panels made of a blend of organic debris and resin that proved to be a good food source for hungry rodents.

Wikipedia's factual history of the car includes many unintentionally funny facts, the sort of details that are absolutely essential in writing fondly humorous pieces.

Humor, of course, is not the same as the snarkiness typical to social media addicts, people who came of age immersed in irony and who think that nasty comments are both practical and entertaining.

"A forty-minute wait and the worst service I have ever experienced" doesn't provide much helpful context, nor does it establish credibility for the writer. Simply because you've posted a couple of dozen slasher comments on Facebook doesn't make you a critic.

To write authoritatively, reviewers and critics must have deep experience in their fields. Simply gushing "I love this car" or "I hate this car" isn't a review—it's an emotional response that must be included under the large umbrella of history, comparison, subjective reaction, and objective evaluation.

Blending pertinent elements in a flowing narrative is an aspirational high art for reviewers of all varieties:

The ZoomBuggy 552 is incredibly fun to drive, cheap to operate, and comes packed with enough technology to fill a NASA control center. We tell you how it handles long straightaways, narrow mountain switchbacks, and urban gridlock.

That's something every car buyer would like to read.

Chapter 33

BASICS OF REVIEWING, PART 2: RESTAURANTS

Recently opened in a repurposed industrial site, Marissa's Mambo is on the inside track to become this city's next top eatery. Its warm, low-key décor belies an adventurous menu, a globe-spanning exercise in fusion cuisine.

Protégée of legendary culinary artist Nikolai Pancetti, chef Marissa Cabrerra has combined her experience growing up in disparate places throughout the world— her parents were in the diplomatic corps—with a playful sense of unexpected juxtapositions. Her flayed calamari with a cumin-and-curry pistachio dusting is a good introduction and pairs exceptionally well with her citrus salad and cornbread fritters. The wine selection is equally pan-global, with vintages varying from surprisingly delicious and affordable to exotic and challenging...

Are you a "foodie"—someone with a passion for kitchens and cuisine? Could your passion sustain you through writing reviews of restaurants? Would writing diminish or enhance your love affair with food? If you're inclined to answer "enhance," read on. Almost everyone *is* a foodie to some extent, but very few are motivated enough to write about it.

For those who do, reviewing restaurants can be a great way to develop an entertaining journalistic style—and to explore food and drink they may otherwise never have encountered.

There is always a need for insightful coverage of restaurants, and not nearly enough gourmands with journalistic skill to fill that need, but don't be deceived into thinking that reviewing includes postings on Facebook—"*Jumping Jill's* onion-and-sweet-potato pancakes are 2Die4!"

That's an enthusiastic endorsement, but it's not a review, and other than adding one more thumbs-up to *Jumping Jill's*, it doesn't provide much helpful information for potential visitors.

A helpful review includes a sketch of the restaurant's history, a description of its exterior and interior, some biographical tidbits about the chef, and maybe a couple of comments from the restaurant's owner/manager about its place in the culinary ecosystem.

You also need to mention hours, location, and accessibility. Is it easy to reach by public transit or only by car? Is there plenty of parking? Is the neighborhood safe and well lit? Is the place crowded and noisy, or cozy and quiet? What sort of music gets played? Live or recorded, or a combination of the two? Are there TVs with sporting events at the bar? Does the restaurant have a happy hour? If so, does it offer a sample platter or small plates?

Restaurants work toward several simultaneous purposes not shared by other cultural institutions: eating is a necessity, of course, but it's also the most popular form of entertainment. Gathering around food is perhaps our oldest social institution. So, covering culinary arts is a journalistic "evergreen" (a niche that will always need skilled writers), much as cookbooks are a publishing evergreen. People who really enjoy the art of food are always eager to read more about it.

In addition to reading the works of current food writers, potential culinary critics would do well to delve into the field's history. Decades before Anthony Bourdain conceived his *Parts Unknown* television series, M.F.K. Fisher wrote enormously insightful and entertaining food-centric travelogues.

Familiarity with the work of Fisher and Bourdain is basic training for aspiring restaurant critics. To make a meaningful statement about where we are, we need to know where we've been.

Chapter 34

BASICS OF REVIEWING, PART 3: ART

V isual art is a luxury enterprise. Art lovers may assert that it's a psychological necessity, but even the most ardent will admit that no one starves for lack of art.

In fact, we are not "starved" for it at all. We are overwhelmed by it. The world is full of artists at all levels, from novice hobbyists to career professionals. Together, they generate more work than there is room to display it. This is why cafés and coffee shops function as third- or fourth-tier art galleries. By offering display space to local artists, they provide opportunities for exposure that artists and potential fans might not have.

Visual art has been part of human culture since the days of cave-dwellers. It predates written language by thousands of years. It became formalized with the advent of civilization and was typically used to convey political and religious themes and to glorify the ruling class, often depicted in flattering, yet not overly realistic, sculptures and portraits.

Art's historic function of realistic depiction—basically, a method of visual record-keeping—was usurped by photography as it gained traction in the mid-nineteenth century, prompting artists to explore new forms of expression, such as impressionism, a style of painting that's as much about the feel of a scene as it is about how it looks.

Some conservative art historians think that impressionism was both the high point and the last gasp of Western culture, but others see it as the gestation period for the creative explosion that happened in the twentieth century and continues today.

As a critic, you need to become comfortable with terms such as cubism, modernism, postmodernism, pop art, abstract expressionism, socialist realism, and related hybrids and subgenres. Simply knowing a bit about da Vinci and Rembrandt won't get you very far, nor will tossing out a few conversational tidbits about Andy Warhol. That would be like having a few phrases of high school French and imagining that you could converse in Paris.

Intensely fascinating and sometimes troubling, art is an arena where there is always room for informed and passionate discussion. If you have insatiable curiosity and boundless enthusiasm for the subject, you'll soon find a niche in the art-world ecosystem.

That said, as with writing about cars or cuisine or any other subject, one doesn't simply wade into art criticism without some background.

This doesn't imply a degree in art history or experience making art, although both would be hugely helpful, but it does mean familiarity with the field. If you're uncertain about terms such as *pastoral* and *figurative* or *realism* and *abstraction*, you've got some research to do. If spending hours in museums and galleries is your definition of excruciating boredom, it may be research you don't want to do. In fact, if that describes you, then art is definitely not your future.

On the other hand, you may be that rare specimen who gains energy visiting museums, who eagerly anticipates new gallery exhibits, and who pays close attention to developments in the art community.

If you're already a reader of journals such as *Art in America* and *Art News*, and a subscriber to *Art Net*, you're way ahead of the game and may be a perfect candidate to become an art critic.

Chapter 35

BASICS OF REVIEWING, PART 4: VISITING A GALLERY

I magine that you are a newbie art critic about to launch yourself into the reviewing game.

You want to cover a new exhibit at the Serpentine Gallery, a startup in your city's trendiest district. Perhaps you discovered it through a mass email or by accident while walking by. What prompted you to visit? Was it an intriguing press release or a couple of baffling photos? Or was it the bustling business of installing the show that you witnessed as you strolled by?

You might be tempted to visit the Serpentine on the exhibit's opening night, when the featured artist will be there. That might provide an opportunity to grab a couple of pithy quotes from the artist, the gallerist, and a few attendees. Still, it won't give you a chance to really view the art, because in all likelihood, the place will be crowded to the point of inducing panic attacks. If the crowd doesn't bother you, please enjoy the wine, cheese, crackers, and baby carrots. Just keep it all close to the vest—jostling and spills are likely.

Opening night lets you rub elbows, literally, with dozens of artists and art lovers, but to really absorb what this exhibit is all about, you'll need to come back during the day, when the gallery is relatively empty. Then, you can spend as much time as you wish with each piece.

Newcomers may feel more confident having done some research before venturing in. Still, the opposite tack is equally effective: go in knowing as little as possible so you can have an unsullied experience, both intellectually and emotionally. Your reactions are valid regardless of your expertise or credentials. You can always read up on your subject later—and if you are so motivated, revisit the exhibit with new knowledge.

Your review might run 500-700 words, about one or two pages on most websites or local newspapers, with room for a couple of good photos, or 1,200 words if it's a more in-depth piece. It might also be much shorter, even a single paragraph, such as the capsule reviews of gallery exhibits, movies, plays, etc., that appear in *The New Yorker*.

Reading and writing capsule reviews are excellent training because they force you to condense as much information as possible into a tight space. If you're writing for an online outlet—almost everyone is today—remember that even though there is no practical length limit, the internet is a short-attention-span medium. Your work will be better received if it is concise.

Regardless of the length of your piece, essential info includes tidbits about the gallery and its owner, the neighborhood, and, obviously, the artists and their work. Thus:

Recently opened in a former shoe store on East River Street, the Serpentine Gallery has launched its inaugural exhibit featuring new works by painter Savanna Maguire, whose promising, if sometimes problematic, career was interrupted by the demands of caring for her two young children, now old enough to spend their days in school.

Enforced inactivity hasn't diminished Maguire's considerable talents—in fact, her return to the studio has proven to be quite a revelation. Her political posturing and pent-up need to paint have been leavened by motherhood and by the imaginative kinetics of her son and daughter.

Formerly known for sharp, bitter imagery, Maguire has acquired a gentler tone in the new series, many of which are figurative abstracts inspired by her children and their friends and activities. The stark reds, blacks, and jagged angles of her earlier work have yielded to a warmer palette of sunny gardens and romping children.

Many of Maguire's pieces at the Serpentine are both roughly and expertly rendered, with imagery and texture that combine to pull you into the scene and likewise invite you back.

Most would play well long-term in a wide variety of environments. Her "Day at the Beach #5" is both a riot of color and a dose of familial reassurance; her "Saturnalia" is a delightfully out-of-focus depiction of a backyard birthday party run wild.

"Savanna's artistic evolution has been quite startling,"
says Serpentine owner Samantha Baxter. "She's gone
from angry and indignant to a benevolent fountain of
love and understanding. I would never have thought that
kids could have that effect—they certainly wouldn't for
me—but for Savanna, they've been life-altering."

Her paintings could prove life-altering for some
Serpentine visitors, too.

Evolution: Recent Works by Savanna Maguire

April 1 through May 30
Serpentine Gallery, 145 East River Street
Hours: 10 a.m.—6 p.m. Wednesday through Sunday.
Other hours by appointment.

Chapter 36

BASICS OF REVIEWING, PART 5: MOVIES AND PLAYS

I t's quite likely that in your writing career, you'll have the opportunity to review movies and plays.

These two storytelling art forms are as closely related as first cousins and have influenced each other since the days of silent film. Many films have been based on stage plays, and some stage plays have inspired films. Both, of course, have been inspired by novels, histories, short stories, memoirs, poems, folklore, and even news reports.

Their differences are pretty remarkable, too. Once a film is complete ("in the can," as the industry phrase has it), it's a permanent, unchanging performance—unless, of course, it's subsequently reissued as a director's cut.

Some people consider the original commercial release of *Blade Runner* the finest version. In contrast, others prefer director Ridley Scott's revision, which omits the narration he felt hampered the film's dramatic impact. In either case, your interpretation may change with multiple viewings, but the story and its presentation remain intact. All that can change is your perception.

Stage plays are more malleable because different theater companies may give the same script vastly different treatments. Cast, technical talent, venue, budget, and many other factors, including the prevailing political climate, figure into how a play is presented and how it's received. The audience itself can affect a play, because actors can feel the audience's response, something clearly impossible in a movie theater. Stage actors have long noted that Friday night crowds react differently from Saturday night crowds, especially with comedies.

As a reviewer, you too will be affected by audience responses, as you should be, and your agreement or disagreement with the crowd should find its way into your reviews. You may be baffled why people laughed at a scene you thought was decidedly un-funny. On the other hand, your general harmony with the crowd may reinforce your feeling that your perceptions are correct.

A good critic becomes a trusted guide for readers and, over time, a valuable asset to commercial publications. Some critics, such as film critic Joe Morgenstern or theater critic Terry Teachout (both formerly with the *Wall Street Journal*), become celebrities themselves, with legions of loyal readers.

Well-written reviews are themselves entertaining art forms— and sometimes, reviews can be more enjoyable than the subjects they cover.

Your purpose is to inform readers whether any production, filmed or live, is worthy of patronage. Cost is an essential difference between movies and stage plays—the price of movie tickets is negligible, even during a first run. The cost of watching a film on television or online can sometimes approach zero.

Ticket prices for stage plays are all over the map, from $15 or $20 at community theater companies to many hundreds of dollars for blockbuster Broadway productions. Ease of access and cost of admission must figure into your evaluation, very much the way you would hold a high school football game to a different standard than an NFL game.

Every film or play can be boiled down to its essentials—the 2004 sci-fi thriller *I, Robot* might be described as "Rogue cop battles threatening androids," while *Hamlet*, Shakespeare's enduring tragedy, might be described as "Brooding prince plots revenge for his father's murder."

Shakespeare scholars may be outraged because *Hamlet* encompasses much more than a simple revenge story, but at its core, that's what it is. Likewise, *King Lear* can be boiled down to "All hell breaks loose when an addled monarch divides his kingdom among his three daughters."

Your review needs to cover many aspects of the film or play as succinctly as possible: What's it all about? Who's in it? Where is it being presented? Is it well-paced? Are the actors consistently believable, or are some clearly better than others? Who—or what— stands out? What's the takeaway?

You need to cover more than the story and characters, too, with insightful mentions of staging, set design, cinematography, music, costumes, and more. Minor characters who shine in their roles deserve praise, and major players who disappoint deserve to be called out, regardless of their popularity. Consistent or inconsistent dramatic quality is rightfully attributed to the director. You need to mention this.

Ultimately, is the film or play a good use of time and money?

This is obviously a subjective call, but one you can make confidently if you've covered all the relevant territory. See enough and write enough, and eventually you'll acquire an imposing blend of gravitas, journalistic swagger, and maybe a reputation of your own to rival some of the stars you write about.

It all comes with experience—one review at a time, over the years. Nobody ever promised that you could leap into the game at a high level. We all come into it as beginners.

Chapter 37

BASICS OF REVIEWING, PART 6: THE ART OF DIPLOMACY

Reviews of all kinds are intended to inform consumers about whether something is a good use of their time and money: products, services, entertainment, books, and more.

Trusted reviewers build a following through a combination of expertise and ability to convey critical information as effectively, honestly, and often as humorously as possible. Bloggers and Internet influencers erroneously believe that cursory approval (or dismissal) constitutes an encompassing review. Your readers want to know what's right and what's wrong with the subject of interest, and why. They want details that only experts can provide.

Even the most dismissive review should take an even-handed approach. You may wish to write a cathartic, excoriating screed. It may be fun to write and fun to read, but if you want to be taken seriously, you need to leaven your negative reaction with some positive commentary. That's the nature of diplomacy.

Here's my August 19, 2022, *Aisle Seat Review* coverage of an acclaimed national touring production of the classic mid-century musical *Oklahoma!* The young director altered both the script and the traditional presentation to make the play a bitterly ironic statement about American culture and life in a frontier territory. That was a grave mistake, but the production was well done. This had to be acknowledged, as it would be in any respectable review.

"Nasty, Disjointed "Oklahoma!" Lands in San Francisco"
By Barry Willis

Rodgers and Hammerstein's "Oklahoma!" must have been a deeply traumatic event in the young life of director Daniel Fish.

There's no other explanation for his nasty, disjointed interpretation of the beloved 1950s musical. A small part celebration, a larger part attack, but mostly a personal exorcism, Fish's national touring production opened Wednesday, August 17, to a nearly full house in San Francisco's capacious Golden Gate Theatre.

Entering the theater, the audience squinted into a broad bank of harsh bright lights from high above the stage, perhaps a forewarning that they were about to undergo psychological torment of the type dished out to political prisoners. Below these lights lay the set for the entire production: a huge open room filled with rows of picnic tables and walls festooned with mounted guns—dozens of rifles and shotguns, implying that the space is possibly a hunting club, but also perhaps the rec room of a church, or a school cafeteria. It's a community meeting space with lots and lots of guns.

Gun culture is established early in the show—this is Oklahoma, of course—and despite the story's lack of gunplay, it provides thematic background throughout a nearly three-hour performance. Russian novelist/playwright Anton Chekhov famously commented, "If there's a gun hanging on the wall in act one...you must fire the gun by act three," advice clearly followed by Fish in his rewriting of the show's closing moments.

In the opening scene, we meet most of the pertinent characters near the town of Claremore, Oklahoma Territory, all presided over by matriarch Aunt Eller (Barbara Walsh). This introduction closely adheres to Hammerstein's original, with cowboy Curly (Sean Grandillo) accompanying himself on guitar while singing "Oh, What a Beautiful Morning."

We meet Laurey (Sasha Hutchings), the girl of his dreams, and Jud Fry (Christopher Bannon), village idiot and Curly's rival for Laurey, goofy adventurer Will (Hennesey Winkler), and pivotal comic-relief character Ado Annie (Sis), the "girl who cain't say no." They're mostly in fine voice, especially Sis, blessed with superb comic timing and a powerful contralto. The Laurey/Curly duet "People Will Say We're in Love" is delightful.

But our short stay in traditional romantic musical territory is abruptly ended by a lengthy blackout scene in which Curly and Jud have a man-to-man discussion. The blackout is as annoying and unjustifiable as the airfield landing lights that illuminate the theater on entering, and is inexplicably repeated in the second act. If one long blackout wasn't enough, how about two or three?

The original production featured a "dream ballet" in which Laurey tries to sort out her feelings for Curly and Jud. That's been jettisoned for a solo modern dance routine done to a high-intensity heavy-metal medley of "Oklahoma!" tunes, in the midst of more stage smoke than ever obscured a 1980s rock concert.

Clad in an oversized T–shirt emblazoned with the words "Dream Baby Dream," dancer Jordan Wynn performs well even if John Heginbotham's choreography bears no relationship to 1906 Oklahoma, or to the rest of the show. It's also Wynn's only appearance. Benj Mirman does a nice turn as Ali Hakim, the "Persian" peddler, as does Mitch Tebo as jurist Andrew Carnes. The production's dozen or so musicians are excellent, and the show's actors overall are very good.

As done originally, both stage and film, "Oklahoma!" is a lightweight musical hampered by a weak story—its weakness forgivable because great music carries the show. Fish makes the too-obvious mistake of trying to push "Oklahoma!" into dramatic territory that would have appalled both its authors and previous generations of musical theater fans.

In the original, Jud appears in the penultimate scene at the wedding of Laurey and Curly. He's drunk and belligerent, provokes a fistfight with Curly, then dies after falling on his own knife—an accidental death.

In Fish's version, he arrives stone cold sober, with a wedding gift for Curly: a revolver whose grip he puts in Curly's hands. He provokes the inevitable single shot that kills him, and the blood-spattered newlyweds then sing the "Oklahoma!" anthem as off-key and ironically as possible. It's an intentional abomination.

Fish may have many good reasons for hating the musical, for hating gun culture, for hating the state of Oklahoma and its history. He may even have some good reasons for sympathizing with a character as repellent as Jud Fry, but there's no justification for turning what's basically an upbeat romantic fantasy into a screed about evil.

This "Oklahoma!" is little more than a protracted, self-indulgent exercise in millennial irony. Professional tastemakers in New York and elsewhere may have gushed about its brilliance, but there are certain theatrical icons that should be off-limits to reinterpretation.

Fish's "Oklahoma!" neither honors the original nor does it provide any degree of satisfaction for an audience eager to leave the theater with songs in their hearts. Instead they go home sorry that they paid to be insulted.

Chapter 38

BASICS OF REVIEWING, PART 7: A RAVE REVIEW

Sometimes reviewers are lucky enough to enjoy a production so well-conceived and so well done that there's almost no need for any negative commentary. Such productions deserve all the praise we can heap on them. They make our work a joy.

Below is a review of just such a production: the San Francisco Playhouse's *The Curious Incident of the Dog in the Night-Time*, which ran for approximately six weeks in spring 2025. The review appeared in the May 10, 2025, edition of the *Stage & Cinema* website

"A Stellar "Curious Incident" at San Francisco Playhouse"
By Barry Willis

On rare occasions even the most seasoned reviewers are confounded by the inadequacy of language to describe

a production so beautiful and transcendent that words fail to do it justice.

Such a production is multiple award-winning "The Curious Incident of the Dog in the Night-Time" which opened May 7 at San Francisco Playhouse. It's enjoying a deservedly long run through June 21.

The tale revolves around Christopher Boone, a 15-year-old autistic British kid who discovers that a neighbor's dog has been killed, and sets out to solve the mystery of who did it and why. The stage play by Simon Stephens is based on the novel of the same name, written by Mark Haddon.

A difficult tale to convey—this critic has seen only one previous production, done primarily as a modern dance exercise—the SF Playhouse production excels in every aspect: casting, performance, pacing, set design, sound, lighting and projections. It would be hard to imagine a better presentation. The production takes the audience from dismay to elation in two supremely well-crafted acts.

The opening scene is shocking, with Christopher (Brendan Looney) discovering the carcass of Wellington the dog, skewered with a garden fork. It's the show's only repulsive image, but an essential one, in a fantastically engaging production directed by Susi Damilano.

Mathematically gifted but socially awkward, Christopher has rarely ventured out of his neighborhood other than to go to school, but his determination to discover what happened to Wellington forces him to confront his own fears and limitations, leading to the revelation that his mother, Judy (Liz Sklar), isn't dead, as his father, Ed (Mark P. Robinson), has told him, but instead has been sending him letters from her new residence in London.

Accompanied by his pet rat, Toby, and equipped with only a notebook, a sleeping bag, and a Swiss Army knife, Christopher forces himself to get on the train, something he's never done, and rides into the city in search of her.

The questions he asks of various officials and passersby make little sense to them but are perfectly logical for him. He can't bear being touched and can't use a toilet unless it's been cleaned first. When stressed, he's apt to recite prime numbers ("1, 3, 5, 7, 11…") or cubes ("4, 9, 16, 25…") to calm down. A real autistic himself, Looney encompasses all that makes his character unique and appealing. His performance is an unassailable argument for authenticity in casting. The show's dramaturg, Joel Moore, is cited as being "on the spectrum" too. The alternate reality of such folk has rarely been depicted so well, or with such sympathy and grace.

Projections by Sarah Phykitt fill the back of the stage and are incredibly effective in conveying not only Christopher's mindset—computer games, algebraic formulae, the night sky—but also the landscape whirring past the train and the claustrophobic nature of riding the "tube" in the city.

Phykitt's work is amazing, reinforced by superb sound effects from James Ard. The elegant set by Bill English consists of movable frames outlined in light, used by the cast to perform oddly appropriate and oddly compelling dance moves created by movement director Bridgette Loriaux, whose credits include performing as an aerialist at the Beijing Olympics.

Sophia Alawi is outstanding as Siobhan, Christopher's teacher. Whit K. Lee, Cassidy Brown, Catherine Luedtke, Wiley Naman Strasser, Renee Rogoff, and Laura Domingo are the supporting cast. They are exemplary, most in multiple roles. Quick-change costumes by Alice Ruiz add enormously to the show's pacing and differentiation of characters.

This "Curious Incident" is a reluctant hero's journey, an overwhelming redemption story, and a revelation about the power of theater. It's a celebration of the triumph of the human spirit and an antidote to an art form often saturated with irony and cynicism.

At each performance, the audience is reminded that San Francisco Playhouse is an "empathy gym," a force for good in a world overrun with evil. This production in particular proves beyond doubt the veracity of that assertion. "The Curious Incident" is likely the most life-affirming stage production you will ever see.

"The Curious Incident of the Dog in the Night-Time"

Through June 21
San Francisco Playhouse
450 Post Street, San Francisco
Tickets: $35–$135
Info: 415-677-9596, sfplayhouse.org

* * * *

Barry Willis is a member of the American Theatre Critics Association and president of the San Francisco Bay Area Theatre Critics Circle. Contact: barry.m.willis@gmail.com

THE VALUE OF MENTORSHIP

In 1999, during the first wave of dot-com hysteria, I worked as content director at an audio-and-music startup called *Audiocafe.com*, on Mission Street in San Francisco. "Content-Commerce-Community"—anyone remember that mantra? *Audiocafe.com* was among the 99% of startups that tanked within 18 months of their launch, but during its short life, it was a fun, but very bumpy, ride.

I shared a cubicle with our editor, Clare, a recent graduate of San Francisco State University's journalism school. She was a fine writer and editor whose work had appeared in *Wired* and other journals. Our job was to generate product and music reviews and ensure that everything on the website was concise, literate, informative, and entertaining.

One day, Clare suggested that we recruit some interns to help with content. She leveraged her connections at SF State, identified five promising students, and arranged for them to receive class credit for their contributions. We picked three of the five—one girl and two guys—who began submitting pieces to us.

One day in the office, one of the guys, Mike, asked me for assignment ideas.

"You have some favorite bands, don't you?" I asked.

"Oh yeah, of course," he replied. "I've got tickets to Massive Meltdown at the Concord Pavilion this weekend."

"Great," I said. "You work up a review of the concert, and we'll run it."

He left pumped up with enthusiasm. A dream gig: writing about his favorite band! He got back to me the following Tuesday with something like this:

> *Late last Saturday afternoon, we drove out to Concord Pavilion, got a good parking spot, then made our way through the turnstiles and found our seats. We were eager to see Massive Meltdown, who hadn't played the Bay Area in more than two years.*
>
> *The crowd was rowdy as warm-up act Lust Bucket took the stage. Their first song was "I Wanna Be Your Pitbull," and the second one was "Stomp on My Toes." Then they played "Dysentery" with a long instrumental break and followed that with "Sticky Dewdrops," a new song that will be included in their next album. They followed that with "Puddle of Blood," their most well-known song, with a screaming solo by guitarist Steven Bumblefork.*

Mike's this-happened-then-that-happened linear narrative continued at unjustifiable length, with little distinction between the event's important aspects and its piddling details. We didn't really need to know what he bought at the concession stand during intermission or how long he had to wait to use the restroom.

Many paragraphs into it, he finally mentioned the headliners, his whole reason for going to the Concord Pavilion. His coverage of Massive Meltdown continued in the vein of they-did-this-then-did-that, but buried in his linear recitation were mentions of performance, song selection, staging, presentation, crowd reaction, and fanboy tidbits about the band.

He was watching me with great anticipation as I scanned his piece. *"Oh, my effing god,"* I thought. *"Four years of J-school and this is what he produces. WTF are his parents paying for?"*

I didn't say that to him, of course. Instead, I said, "Mike, this is pretty good, but I see some spots that could use a bit of editing. Let me work on it, and I'll get back to you."

That night, I deconstructed what he had given me, pulling out the juicy salient parts about Massive Meltdown, moving them up front in the piece, giving Lust Bucket secondary mention, and throwing in some of his observations as spice to give readers a feel for what it was like to be in Concord Pavilion for the event.

His original was the equivalent of a plot synopsis masquerading as a film review, but the final version was what I had asked for—a review of the Massive Meltdown concert, an enthusiastic piece that might tweak the interests of other music fans not as enamored of the band as Mike was.

When he was back in the office, I showed him what I had done and explained why. As he read the finished piece, he got tears in his eyes and said, "No one has ever shown me how to do this. I can't thank you enough."

That was actually one of the most satisfying moments of my time at *Audiocafe.com*. I will never understand how Mike got through four years of journalism school without learning how to structure a story, without knowing what to emphasize, what to downplay, and what to ignore, but I felt great about having helped him. I hope that in some small way I encouraged him to keep writing.

I also hope that *Foundation* encourages you to do so.

Be well.

ABOUT THE AUTHOR

Barry M. Willis is a theater critic and arts writer with the *Marin Independent Journal*, Marin County's daily newspaper. Since 2007, he has worked as American correspondent for British audio-and-music journal *Hi-Fi News*, the oldest and most respected such journal in the United Kingdom, to which he provides a monthly opinion column and feature stories.

Formerly executive editor of Northern California theater-and-arts website *Aisle Seat Review* for ten years, Barry now contributes to the Los Angeles-based website *Stage and Cinema*.

A member of the American Theatre Critics Association, he serves as president of the San Francisco Bay Area Theatre Critics Circle, a collegial organization devoted to promoting and recognizing excellence in theatrical arts.

For approximately two decades, Barry was a contributing editor for *Stereophile*, the premier American audio journal. He was also a prolific contributor to *Stereophile's* sister publications, *Guide to Home Theater*, *Ultimate AV*, and *Audio Video Interiors*, and to their respective websites, in addition to providing news coverage for *Home Theater* and *Photographic* magazines.

In 2005, he joined audiophile journal *The Absolute Sound* as news editor, and its sister publication *The Perfect Vision* as section editor for custom installation. He was also a frequent contributor to *DTV* magazine, covering new technology and emerging entertainment.

He has also done considerable work for technology clients, including PBN Audio, Silverline Audio, High Emotion Audio, Crutchfield, Samsung, Sony, LG Electronics, Intersil, and Daniel Hertz S.A.

Barry was an occasional contributor to *Food Arts*, the international journal of the fine dining industry. In 2006, he was nominated for a James Beard Award for Excellence in Journalism by *Food Arts*.

Mr. Willis resides in Sonoma County, California.

www.ingramcontent.com/pod-product-compliance
Lightning Source LLC
Chambersburg PA
CBHW032112280326
41933CB00009B/801